MARKETING HUMAN
SERVICE INNOVATIONS

Volume 146, Sage Library of Social Research

RECENT VOLUMES IN
SAGE LIBRARY OF SOCIAL RESEARCH

MARKETING HUMAN SERVICE INNOVATIONS

Jack Rothman
Joseph G. Teresa
Terrence L. Kay
Gershom Clark Morningstar

Volume 146
SAGE LIBRARY OF
SOCIAL RESEARCH

SAGE PUBLICATIONS
Beverly Hills / London / New Delhi

For information address:

SAGE Publications, Inc.
275 South Beverly Drive
Beverly Hills, California 90212

SAGE Publications India Pvt. Ltd.
C-236 Defence Colony
New Delhi 110 024, India

SAGE Publications Ltd
28 Banner Street
London EC1Y 8QE, England

Printed in the United States of America

Library of Congress Cataloging in Publication Data

Main entry under title:

Marketing human service innovations.

(Sage library of social research ; v. 146)
Bibliography: p.
Includes indexes.
1. Marketing—Social aspects.   2. Corporations,
Nonprofit.   3. Social service—Marketing.   I. Rothman,
Jack.   II. Series.
HF5415.D4882   1983   658.8'02   82-24089
ISBN 0-8039-1964-6
ISBN 0-8039-1965-4 (pbk.)

FIRST PRINTING

CONTENTS

PART I

A SOCIAL MARKETING PERSPECTIVE

CHAPTER 1

INTENTIONS AND OUTCOMES
An Academic Executive Summary

In a work of fiction, you, the reader, are ordinarily asked by the author to experience rather than to analyze. You may then sit back and let the author's words pass by your eyes as he or she sets forth ideas, which may be rational or preposterous, and builds a montage based on those ideas and images to guide you through an obstacle course of complications, leading you, finally, to some sort of insight or new world view.

Wading through a work of nonfiction in the natural or social sciences is more demanding, and far greater cognitive pressures are placed upon you. You are expected to examine critically new ideas you encounter. You are expected to challenge the premises upon which the work is based. You are expected to approach the interpretation of findings and the conclusions that result from such interpretations with a reasoned and disciplined skepticism.

A book concerning innovative formulations adds yet another burden: You are expected to tolerate the peculiarities of the authors in their approach to the format of the volume and the presentation of their "offbeat" concepts. Here, we will seek to be of some help—and that is the purpose of this introductory chapter. We shall provide you with a road map, of sorts, through the maze of speculations, activities, and research results we shall present. It is our hope that this early overview will provide you with a clear sense of our intentions, our rationale for proceeding as we did, a clue to the logic of our design and the procedures we use (some of them necessarily detailed), and some of our general findings.

You may think of this chapter as an academic variation of the "executive summary," often used in policy research and familiar to the readers of government or corporate reports. As our research has strong policy (or at least pragmatic) implications, our approach is in conformance with aspects of current practice.

Some friendly reviewers of our original manuscript expressed in-process curiosity about what we had found out and what it all meant. They indicated, as they read along, some eagerness to learn about what we had ultimately discovered without having to wait for the ever-revealing last chapter. They felt that there were important facts and insights provided at the end, foreknowledge of which would have enriched their understanding of the social marketing methodology we are setting forth. They also believed that a preview would be useful because of the complex and multifaceted nature of the research design and the scope of the procedures and activities carried out.

As advocates and supporters of the concept of feedback, we yielded readily to the wisdom of these observations and constructed this summary chapter. In it we will set forth, simply and broadly, our approach and major findings. We will reserve the bulk of the text of subsequent chapters for detail, elaboration, and interpretation. Some years ago, a company marketed a single LP record containing the "100 greatest masterpieces of classical music—with all the boring parts cut out." If you like, you may think of this chapter as being something akin to that record.

In addition, we will do our best to assist your understanding as we work our way through the book by presenting brief summaries of chapter content at the beginning of each chapter. This is a concession to the principle that redundancy is among the most powerful pedigogical techniques.

In this book we will merge or interrelate two schools of research and theory: the "Diffusion School," which has been developed mainly by sociologists and psychologists, and the "Social Marketing School," which has grown from the field of business. While the fields have been separate, almost airtight in their compartmentalization, their objectives and many of their methods overlap, as we shall demonstrate. Both are concerned with the dissemination and utilization of innovations—new products, techniques, ideas, programs. The difference is that the diffusion people approach their subject from a humanistic or nonprofit point of view, while the social marketing writers draw upon a body of literature that originally had overriding profit-making motivations. The differences have made close similarities appear to be distant incompatibilities.

Philip Kotler, who may be considered the "father" of social marketing, and others from the field of business have come to realize that the techniques and methods evolved in the marketing field can be applied, as well, to social causes, social movements, and philanthropic organizations. At that point diffusion and social marketing, as areas of study, meld.

A point of interest is that the marketing researchers and practitioners have been at work for a longer time, have devoted immeasurably greater resources to it, and have achieved a higher degree of sophistication. They have a great deal to contribute to diffusion theorists and researchers.

The problem is that the fields are so disparate in atmosphere, quality, and ostensible immediate purpose (money versus human development) that diffusion specialists are rather deaf and blind to what can be learned from the social marketing professionals. We believe that social marketing knowledge must be transferred with discernment and sensitivity to the requirements and normative quality of a new field, but that knowledge should be acknowledged and exploited rather than ignored and squandered.

In this book we will define and describe social marketing and illustrate its practical and theoretical relevance to scholars and operational people in diffusion of innovations. As stated by Kotler (1975, p. 282):

Social marketing provides a rich conceptual system for thinking through the problems of bringing about changes in the ideas or practices of a target public. . . . The adoption of an idea, like the adoption of any product, requires a deep understanding of the needs, perceptions, preferences, reference groups, and behavioral patterns of the target audience, and the tailoring of messages, media "costs" and facilities to maximize the ease of adopting the idea.

It is possible to define diffusion in quite identical terms.

Approaching "Social Marketing": A Preview

In the chapters that follow we will describe the development, packaging, and distribution of a particular product, a handbook, intended for use by professionals in the mental health field. It introduced them to new techniques and strategies for dealing with organizational and community aspects of mental health service provision. Specifically, it was intended for workers in community mental health centers and family service agencies and included illustrations from counterpart colleagues. The handbook was the result of a decade-long effort to develop a human services analogue of industrial research and development techniques. We have already discussed that effort at length elsewhere (see University of Michigan, 1977; Rothman, 1974; Rothman et al., 1976, 1977, 1978, 1981), and we will also provide a general background to that effort in the next chapter. Following the inherent logic of the R&D process, a diffusion plan had to be devised to put the materials in the hands of potential users. It is that diffusion aspect of R&D upon which we will be concentrating in this book.

While the social science diffusion literature and the commercial/industrial experience provided us with a general road map of the major problems we could expect along the way, it could not flag for us all the potholes, barriers, and turmoil we would meet as we proceeded toward our goal. Furthermore, much of the ground we would cover was not well traveled; many of the conceptual tools and specific procedures we would need did not exist in the social sciences. For example, the counterpart of the industrial engineer—the social engineer or knowledge linker—did not exist to any extent. Neither did the social counterpart of the detail person, the traveling sales representative, or the advertising account specialist. We had to invent these. As we went along, we encountered continuing surprises. On occasion, too, we found a result that challenged traditional social science notions.[1]

Diffusion methods have been discussed at some length by Rogers and Shoemaker (1971), Zaltman et al. (1973), and others. What their work reveals is that there are a multitude of such approaches. These can be thought of as falling into two broad categories: "high intensity" (personal contact approaches) and "low intensity" (mass communication approaches). High-intensity approaches offer a greater degree of personal interaction, immediate feedback, and focused expertise. They also require a large investment in staff time and financial resources and, ordinarily, cover a smaller number of potential users. Low-intensity techniques reach larger numbers of people and, ordinarily, require fewer resources per contact. The drawback is that they allow less initiative and flexibility in influencing potential users. Litwak (1959), especially, provides us with a cogent discussion of these theoretical perspectives.

As high-intensity approaches are considerably more expensive in terms of human resources, time, travel, facilities, and other costs, not all agencies have the resources to engage in this type of diffusion. Further, such procedures ordinarily sacrifice communication with a larger pool of potential users. Using this larger pool might well result in greater aggregate utilization. In the event that what is communicated is simple or the audience is favorable or highly motivated, low intensity might be the preferred approach.

Clearly, innovations vary in complexity while human service agencies manifest certain ideological preferences, and have variable resources. These and other factors will dictate that such agencies in aggregate will continue to use both approaches. It was, therefore, incumbent upon us to explore both high-intensity and low-intensity approaches and to assess cost-effective variations between the two basic approaches. Our target market in both cases was the professional staff complement of community mental health centers, federally funded by the National Institute of Mental Health (NIMH), and of family service agencies, affiliated with the Family Service Association of America.

In our research we employed both high- and low-intensity approaches for diffusing our handbook to the target market. We conducted a follow-up evaluation for market testing purposes three months after the diffusion treatment. In this follow-up, users were asked to specify their experience with the handbook. We devised a special instrument, the "Depth of Utilization Scale" (DUS) to measure behavioral aspects of handbook use. The DUS was the chief dependent variable used for appraising diffusion/social marketing results.

In our mass communication study, we also employed a "Dissemination Rate" measure. By "dissemination" we mean the amount of mass distribution brought about as a result of mailings (our low-intensity distribution technique). We calculated the rate from the number of orders placed for handbooks by agencies subjected to different treatments. It was an unobtrusive measure, drawn from bookkeeping records of orders received and filled. It is an indicator of distribution (entry into the organization) rather than utilization (the process activated once entry is achieved). Social marketing may be concerned with either or both of these aspects of diffusion.

The Low-Intensity (Mass Communications) Study

According to Rosenau (n.d.), low-intensity or impersonal approaches provide information in a simple and inexpensive way. These approaches are of various kinds: direct mailings to agencies or individual professionals; printed matter delivered by hand through such devices as hang-bags on the recipient's door-knob, a stack of copies at a booth in a convention, delivery in faculty mailboxes, and so on; periodicals distributed by professional associations through newsletters, journals, special issues, and so on. Each method has its advantages and special purposes. Direct mailings, for example, are viewed by Rosenau as suited especially for installing or replacing visible or low-risk innovations. Professional periodicals can offer more detailed information on previous trials.

In our low-intensity program, we used mass mailings to agencies as an intermediate-level mass communication technique (mailings directed at particular agencies are obviously less diffuse than radio broadcasts or newspaper ads, but not as concentrated as printed matter delivered by hand). Two factors may be important in such mass-mailing dissemination—type of reference group appeal to potential users and point of entry into the organization. In other words, in a direct mailing to an organization, one must decide both to which level in the hierarchy the communication should be addressed (the director, middle management, line staff) and the kind of appeal that will catch the attention and motivate the members of that organization (appeals to loyalties to the agency itself, appeals to professional norms, or appeals to the interests and requirements of the clients). We will discuss these factors in detail in Chapter 3 relative to the existing literature. For the purposes of orientation, however, we will touch upon them briefly here.

REFERENCE GROUP APPEALS

Three basic role orientations have been suggested in studies concerning professional workers: *bureaucratic* (or agency), *professional,* and *community/client.* We have observed elsewhere (Rothman, 1974, p. 83):

> In this formulation, professional orientation implies a high concern with professional values and standards, a bureaucratic orientation refers to a preoccupation with policies and norms of the employing agency, and client orientation connotes a primary attention to the needs of those served by the agency.

Research that we will discuss in Chapter 3 suggests that the community/client appeal is not apt to be a very strong one, certainly not as strong as the other two. Existing research also fails to make clear precisely which of the other two is more apt to be the stronger.

For the low-intensity study, the brochures that we had professionally designed to "sell" the handbook in the two target human service systems we were seeking to affect were identical in all respects but one. Each incorporated a separate appeal designed to address what we believed were the reference group identifications of professionals within the service systems. One was a specially designed bureaucratic appeal, one a specially designed professional appeal, and one was specially designed for those whose interests were primarily community/client.

POINTS OF ENTRY

Studies conflict as to whether or not the chief administrator is actually a facilitator of innovations. While in a position to introduce and enforce new procedures and practices, the need to maintain the agency and to respond to a multiplicity of different pressures may encourage a posture of stability rather than of change.

Some research supports the notion that collegial and decentralized decision-making processes may facilitate innovation. This presumes that program people are more open to innovation or more inventive than top-level personnel. Other research, however, argues that resistance by middle-level people may be a major obstacle to the adoption of an innovation. Still other work, particularly that of Litwak et al. (1970) and Fairweather (1974), seems to suggest that diffusion rates may be independent of point of entry. In our research we used both levels of entry, and further subdivided the middle level into training specialists and special interest persons. These considerations point out some elements of strategic planning that need to be taken into account in a diffusion effort.

Our low-intensity study, then, was a 3 X 3 comparison of points of entry against reference group appeals—Executive, Training Specialist, Special Interest Specialist points of entry against Bureaucratic, Professional, Community/Client reference group appeals. The study involved some 600 agencies; approximately 350 were community mental health centers, and approximately 250 were family service agencies.

Better than 40 percent of the agencies ordered handbooks as a result of our direct mailing of the brochure. This resulted in the distribution of about 2700 handbooks to about 50 percent of the family service agencies and 35 percent of the community mental health agencies. About one-fifth of those who received the handbook subsequently reported a "high" level of utilization. Those in family service organizations tended to put it to greater use than those in community mental health centers.

With respect to utilization, the Community/Client appeal had little effect. For community mental health centers, Bureaucratic and Professional appeals were both effective. For family service agencies the trend was for the Bureaucratic appeal in particular to be effective. Variations from this pattern were found for dissemination or distribution as compared to actual utilization.

Point of entry used appeared to make no difference in dissemination and utilization, a finding consistent with several theorists we shall discuss later.

We also looked at the combined effects of entry and appeal. We found that none of the 9 treatment cells combining a particular entry and appeal (in each of which there were approximately 65 agencies) was more significant than any other in promoting utilization.

The High-Intensity Study

High-intensity or "personal selling" methods of diffusion involve direct contact and interaction between the diffusion agent and the receiver of the communication. Rosenau (n.d.) suggests that this approach includes such methods as visitation by potential users to a demonstration site, workshops or training sessions, educational or sales "pitches," and direct visits to individual potential users such as those carried out by pub-lishers' representatives or detail people associated with drug firms. He further suggests that if a package is highly complex, a demonstration may be useful. A workshop can assist in gaining peer support to try out something that is risky. The one-to-one personal visit allows considerable feedback and clarification with regard to an innovation requiring the working through of attitudes or the providing of much information.

In our high-intensity diffusion program, we employed the workshop format. It involved personal contact intensity, but, at the same time, allowed such contact to influence 15 to 20 individuals at one time. In other words, we thought it a cost-effective means of applying high-intensity diffusion. It is also a common and familiar staff development procedure by which professionals learn new techniques in the human services fields.

Where our low-intensity study was built upon a 3 X 3 matrix, our high-intensity study was based upon a 2 X 2. We had two sets of concerns that dictated this structure: the status of the diffusion agent (whether he or she was an authority figure or a professional peer) and the location of the diffusion agent (whether he or she was internal to the agency—that is, a member of the staff—or external to the agency—that is, a professional associated with our research project, either as a primary researcher or a practitioner/implementer of innovative interventions that were field tested). The four conditions, thus, were external peer, internal peer, external authority, and internal authority.

We conducted workshops in some 40 community mental health and family service agencies in 8 urban centers in the eastern and midwestern United States. More than 700 individuals participated in the diffusion program. About half of these 700 completed the follow-up market testing evaluation 3 months later.

Our findings revealed no basic differences between authority figures and professional peers—both were equally effective diffusion agents. Our findings consistently and significantly favored the internal agent, however, over the external agent in the community mental health centers. While the same finding was not significant in the family service agencies, the trend of the results was in the same direction. Indeed, the findings were sufficiently strong to lead us to the conclusion that in dissemination of the *particular type of product or technique* we were concerned with, the internal diffusion agent ought to be relied upon.

Among other findings, we learned that those who filled out reactionnaires immediately following the workshop gave significantly higher favorable responses to the external authority. It appears that the external agent, coming from the outside, may generate more excitement, enthusiasm, and anticipation in the short run.

Comparing the High- and Low-Intensity Approaches

An important and somewhat provocative finding from these two substudies is that the low-intensity mass communications study proved to be more cost-effective than the high-intensity personal contact study. Excluding fixed costs, high-intensity program expenses were approximately double those of the low-intensity program. The high-intensity program reached approximately 700 individuals, while the low-intensity program allowed us to make initial contact with about 2700 mental health professionals. While the high-intensity approach resulted in a higher percentage of "high utilization of the handbook" than the low-intensity approach (30 percent versus 22 percent), in absolute numbers the low-intensity approach resulted in almost twice as many individuals (223 versus 113) employing the handbook guidelines at high levels of utilization. Thus for half the cost the low-intensity approach resulted in twice the amount of substantial utilization. Such a finding, if replicated, of course, has significant (while disconcerting, for some) implications for future diffusion research and for social marketing efforts.

A Concluding Note

In this brief preview of what is to come, we have sketched the shape and substance of this book. It is our hope that as a result the specifics of theory, method, refinements in findings, our own reservations, and the possibilities of our work will be easier to follow. We trust that this introduction will, at the same time, make possible a more interesting and meaningful encounter for you, the reader of this work.

Note

1. The following section is a condensation of a portion of Chapter 10 in Jack Rothman, *Social R&D: Research and Development in the Human Services,* ©1980. Reprinted by permission of Prentice-Hall, Inc., Englewood Cliffs, NJ.

References

Fairweather, G. W., Sanders, D. H., & Tornatzky, L. G. *Creating change in mental health organizations.* New York: Pergamon, 1974.

Kotler, P. *Marketing for non-profit organizations.* Englewood Cliffs, NJ: Prentice-Hall, 1975.

Litwak, E. Some policy implications in communications theory with emphasis on group factors. In Council on Social Work Education, *Education for social work, proceedings of the seventh annual program meeting.* New York: Council on Social Work Education, 1959.

Litwak, E., Figueira-McDonough, J., Agemian, J., Hamilton, G., & Rhoades, G. *Towards the multi-factor theory and practice of linkages between formal organizations.* Washington, DC: Social and Rehabilitation Services Department, U.S. Department of Health, Education and Welfare, 1970.

Rogers, E. M., & Shoemaker, F. F. *Communication of innovations* (2nd ed.). New York: Macmillan, 1971.

Rosenau, F. S. *Tactics for the educational change agent: A preliminary analysis.* Far West Laboratory for Educational Research and Development, San Francisco, no date.

Rothman, J. *Planning and organizing for social change: Action principles from social research.* New York: Columbia University Press, 1974.

Rothman, J. *Social R&D: Research and development in the human services.* Englewood Cliffs, NJ: Prentice-Hall, 1980.

Rothman, J., Erlich, J. L., & Teresa, J. G. *Promoting innovation and change in organizations and communities: A planning manual.* New York: John Wiley, 1976.

Rothman, J., Erlich, J. L., & Teresa, J. G. *Changing organizations and community programs.* Beverly Hills, CA: Sage, 1981.

Rothman, J., Teresa, J. G., & Erlich, J. L. *Developing effective strategies of social intervention: A research and development methodology* (PB-272454 TR-1-D). Springfield, VA: National Technical Information Service, 1977.

Rothman, J., Teresa, J. G., & Erlich, J. L. *Fostering participation and innovation: Handbook for human service professionals.* Itasca, IL: Peacock, 1978. (Formerly *Mastering systems intervention skills,* a publication of the Community Intervention Project, University of Michigan—Ann Arbor.)

University of Michigan, Division of Research Development and Administration. The Community Intervention Project. *Research News,* 1977, 27(6), 17-22.

Zaltman, G., Duncan, R., & Holbeck, J. *Innovations and organizations.* New York: John Wiley, 1973.

CHAPTER 2

UTILIZING KNOWLEDGE
A Problem of Social Marketing

A number of years before Mr. Marconi astonished the world by broadcasting the results of the British Regatta by wireless voice transmission, a tinkerer farmer from Murray, Kentucky—a man named Nathan B. Stubblefield—put on an even more remarkable demonstration in a cornfield. He had none of the awesome electronic apparatus of Marconi, only two metal rods. Each of the rods was pointed at one end. At the other, each had mounted upon it a cigar-box-sized enclosed metal container. Watching his demonstration were two reporters from the Baltimore *Sun* and a handful of low-level Washington bureaucrats. As they looked on, they saw Stubblefield jam one rod into the ground, move away from it a distance of perhaps 200 yards, and there jam the other rod into the ground. Then he called for each of the observers to say something softly into the box nearest him. As they spoke, Stubblefield shouted back at them across the field, repeating word for word what each had said.

Nathan B. Stubblefield had not only discovered AM radio a decade before Marconi, but many electronic researchers now believe he may have discovered FM broadcasting a full half century before Armstrong. Stubblefield was a secretive and suspicious man. Although he patented his device (no. 887, 357), he feared someone would steal his invention from him. There is some evidence that electronic theory did not catch up with Stubblefield's incredible insights until after World War II. The important contributions he might have made were made by others. Society never benefited directly from the fruits of his particular genius because those fruits were never shared.

A Brief Look Forward

In this chapter we discuss the importance of linking research knowledge with practice problems. We examine briefly the nature of research and development in industry as a mechanism for converting and linking basic research with practical application. We suggest that analogues of methods and processes of industrial R&D find application in the social realm to yield an equivalent "social R&D." We assert our belief that social R&D is *one* useful approach in linking the findings of research with the needs of practice, and we discuss how "social products" may be developed through social R&D.

We discuss the need for taking the social product to market, that is, getting it to those whose needs it addresses, examining briefly how such products are diffused through the professional community. Two separate schools of theory and research, diffusion of innovations and social marketing, are described, and their relationships indicated. We then review two approaches we explored in diffusing a particular product—a handbook for mental health professionals—throughout two appropriate professional "markets": community mental health workers, and the professional staff of family service agencies. The two different approaches involve a low-intensity diffusion effort involving the use of mass communications techniques and a high-intensity effort based upon personal contact through professional workshops.

Knowledge Utilization, Innovation, and Diffusion

In this book we are concerned with the creation of innovative tools for the human services fields and, even more, with their widespread dissemination and use. Our interest in the diffusion of innovations has an atypical history for social research and an equally atypical context. These can be seen in previous reports of our work, which center upon identifying analogies between research and development in industry and in the social field.

In the industrial world one finds concerted use of knowledge produced in the physical sciences. Such data are sought after as a valued source for product development. There is a firm linkage between research and the relevant applied world. The social sciences, younger and less developed, have not yielded as rich a pool of verified and agreed-upon knowledge. Thus the linkage between the research on one hand and applied settings and professional services providers on the other is more tenuous. Nevertheless, over the years an impressive body of social science research findings have accumulated. The potential, need-satisfying worth of this body of knowledge is similar in some ways to that amassed in the physical sciences. Both the social sciences and the physical sciences are knowledge-generating enterprises, and the resulting knowledge pools contain the potential for solving problems and meeting needs in their respective realms. It is at this point that the two parallel fields diverge.

In the research-industry/business system, the product of research is fed into some great black box. That black box is called "research and development"—"R&D"—and it is the mechanism that forms a powerful, formal, permanent, effective, and readily identifiable link between the research process and the needs of the marketplace. It is that link between industry and science that makes the system work so well. R&D is an essential secondary industry—the factory that turns the raw material of research into useful, acceptable, need-oriented products. This system for invention has overwhelmed and largely replaced individual geniuses such as Nathan Stubblefield.

For the greater period of its existence, research utilization in the social sciences, comparably, has been little more than a cottage industry. From a procedural standpoint, we in the social sciences still operate in the elegant and more leisurely time frame of the mid-eighteenth century. That which has traditionally linked research and practice in the social sphere has been ephemeral, transcient, and informal. Those of us concerned with the human condition have sorely felt the weakness of this research-practice link. We have not had the advantages of a big black box—not until quite recently. It is our contention that weakness in social science knowledge utilization is not so much due to a lack of exactness as it is due to a lack of linkage.

In the past decade social scientists and human service professionals have begun to examine how the linking mechanism of industrial R&D might be redesigned and adapted to solving social problems—how to insert our own "social R&D" into the research-practice policy system in order to create a stronger, more effective link between them. It seems reasonably clear that if R&D can be translated effectively from the commercial sphere to areas of social concern, powerful "new" tools will become available to both researchers and practitioners. A look inside the black box shows why.

In its most simplified form, R&D is a process by which industry develops products and/or services to meet some predetermined societal need or want. It begins with an examination of research and theory that pertains to the specific need. If the existing body of research is not sufficient, new research is conducted to elicit new information, new concepts, new scientific principles. Next, the relevant information that has been gathered undergoes a conversion and design application process from which emerge, it is hoped, the need-specific products and/or services. These applied design formulations are analyzed for their need-fulfillment potential through performance testing. Such tests may result in further redesign or even the abandonment of a product or service if it fails to do what it is supposed to do or if it is rejected (for whatever rational or irrational reason) by its prospective users or individual entrepreneurs.

When it has been determined that the product or service has the requisite level of need-fulfillment potential and is reliable, feasible, and acceptable, the next phase of activity comes into play. This is the promotional marketing phase, the dissemination or diffusion of the product or service from the producer to the appropriate consumer or user.

Social R&D is designed along lines similar to industrial R&D. Problems and needs identified by human services practitioners direct "social engineers," those who function within our own black box, to the body of social science research relevant to the identified problem or need. Potentially useful information is retrieved from the body of existing research and a consensus of the research findings arrived at. Hopefully, the consensus will be sufficiently strong occasionally to dictate the design that the need-specific problem-solving tool(s) will assume. If the consensus is not sufficiently strong, further research must be done.

The consensus generalizations derived from the body of research must then go through a conversion and design phase, just as they do in industrial R&D. Here, generalizations and theoretical statements are converted into concrete, applicable formulations. These are then "engineered" into a "product" through developmental research. This product is field tested to ascertain both its usefulness and the acceptability of its "design." In social R&D this product will typically take the form of a manual, an instructional audiovisual presentation, a training program, and the like. There is virtually no limit, however, to the variety of forms the product might take.

Alterations in design may well take place as a result of this field test. Further field testing is then required until the product demonstrates its effectiveness in meeting the specified need and gives the requisite promise of acceptability to the potential users (or until it is determined that it does neither of these).

Where social R&D and its accompanying component of social marketing fit structurally into the entire social science research utilization process becomes clear in the following descriptive model of the process. The model was empirically developed from our work in the Community Intervention Project, an ongoing social R&D research program based at the University of Michigan and supported by the National Institute of Mental Health (see Figure 2.1).

The model is a description of the operations involved in the creation and distribution of need-specific practice strategies and tools for human service practitioners, derived from basic social science research. It underwent—and continues to undergo—modification, but it has the audacious virtue of aiming explic-

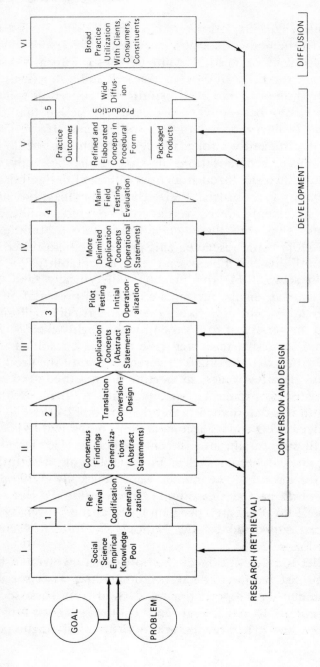

SOURCE: Jack Rothman, SOCIAL R&D: Research and Development in the Human Services, © 1980, p. 23. Reprinted by permission of Prentice-Hall, Inc., Englewood Cliffs, N. J.

Figure 2.1: Schematic Model of Research Utilization—R&D Process

itly and self-consciously to be useful. It is both a descriptive and a prescriptive paradigm. In this instance what we produced was a practical handbook to guide professionals in certain organizational and community interventions. The handbook is described further later in this chapter. It can also be reviewed directly (Rothman et al., 1978).

Of course, social R&D does not make human problem solving easy. Nothing can, given the enormous complexity and indeterminacy of the human condition. What it can do for us—as our own work in the Community Intervention Project (CIP) appears to illustrate—is provide a more guided and more systematic method of developing innovative tools and strategies to employ in social problem solving. Furthermore, the end product of R&D, as a result of incremental testing, is something that has been demonstrated to work. A great deal of trial and error that now occurs in implementing social programs may thus be eliminated. The concrete workings of social R&D have been described and documented in a series of CIP publications (see University of Michigan, 1977; Rothman, 1974; Rothman et al., 1976, 1977, 1978, 1981).

Now we are ready to get back to Nathan Stubblefield. When we began the work of CIP back in the late 1960s, we were motivated by the belief that a resolution of the research-practice dichotomy could be found in the development of strong linking mechanisms between research and practice. We found that the process of social R&D did indeed make possible the development of research-derived practice innovations. Having made this discovery, we assumed, like those who have developed a better mousetrap (or wireless transmitter) that the user world would beat a path to our door. We did not really anticipate in the beginning that innovative product development, in itself, is not a necessary and sufficient condition to effect resolution to the social science research-practice disjuncture. It was only when we had an innovative product in hand that the awful truth dawned on us: We did not know how best to place our product into the hands of human service professionals who had need of it. Some affirmative form of promotional marketing or distribution was required to complete the link. Thus it was that we turned our attention to a critical problem in the entire social science research utilization process: discovering the dynamics that control the marketing process in the human services fields and then applying what is learned to the development of effective marketing strategies.

Just as it is possible to extrapolate from industrial R&D to devise a useful, systematic method of developing new practice tools from research, so, too, is it possible to extrapolate from business marketing practices to guide us in the more effective and timely distribution of these new practice tools. For the purposes of parallel consistency, such extrapolation may be termed "social marketing."

Promotional marketing is a step to which the science-industry system devotes as many effort resources as it does to all other steps in the process combined. It is the step at which industry communicates what it has to its potential customers through a variety of communication tools. It is a step in the social science research utilization process that has traditionally been given insufficient attention. In this presentation we shall focus our discussion of marketing on the diffusion or distribution aspect, although some marketing scholars have approached the notion more broadly to include need fulfillment and project development.

The problem before us is how one communicates with the marketplace so that the research utilization process is carried to a logical and productive conclusion. If the willing suspension of disbelief permits the supposition that social R&D has the capacity for developing effective need-specific tools for social problem solving, what is the best way to get the knowledge of such tools to the proper "consumers" and the tools themselves into their hands? These are the core questions to which we address ourselves in this book.

Using Professional Innovations[1]

The term "product advocacy" conveys the essence of what we are dealing with. Radnor and his associates (1976) speak of product advocacy as embodying an aggressive, energetic strategy of following through on development outcomes. The notion reflects a professionally responsible attitude toward the results of one's action-research efforts. Once an innovation has been created in which the development team has confidence (based on hard evaluation of performance outcomes), it follows that careful and sustained effort will be directed at putting this construction into wide use on behalf of consumers and clients— the intended beneficiaries of human service organizations.

As we shall see, social marketing intersects with the product advocacy concept. Of course, diffusion and social marketing may pertain to any social innovation, whether derived from controlled research, practice experimentation, idiosyncratic innovation, serendipity, or virtually any form of mundane or divine revelation.

In the business world, as we have already noted, the importance of diffusion is well recognized. A variety of code words signify its saliency: marketing, promotion, sales, distribution. Ansoff (1961, p. 209) points out that all research and development work in a business firm is based upon "market-product strategy," a central purpose of which is to "maximize profits over the long run." A number of different roles have been institutionalized in order to implement this aspect: salespersons, detail people, publishers' representatives, and so on. Indeed, one is quite able to conclude that in the commercial sphere this is the tail that wags the entire operation.

For this reason and others, the place of diffusion has been deprecated in the social sciences and the human service professions. It is associated with the crude commercialism of business. In describing their attitudes toward disseminating a mental health innovation, Tornatzky and Fairweather (1976, pp. 11-12) state:

> Unfortunately the role demands of this type of research are quite incongruous with many of the role demands of the traditional academic researcher. In many ways the role that we play is more akin to that of a Willy Loman with a Ph.D.

Guba (1968, p. 53) makes the same point:

> Diffusion is an activity regarded with some distaste by many members of the educational establishment, particularly the research community. It is often equated with hucksterism.

It is certainly not unreasonable that the process of social marketing, because of its commercial antecedents, would at first be viewed with some skepticism by researchers and practitioners alike. Some suspicion of the concept is counseled by more than 500 years of academic tradition. There is a long-standing intellectual convention among serious scholars and academicians, particularly, that counsels the avoidance of any appearance of presumptive behavior with respect to our philosophical or scientific notions. Instead, it is expected that these should be offered to our peers for reflection and examination; and our peers, because they are men and women of rational intellect, will accept that which is consistent with popular intellectual cosmology and reject that which is not. The system has worked well for philosophical thought. It has not worked so well in dealing with matters related to social problem solving.

In a large-scale evaluation of the diffusion effort of the National Institute of Education, the Dissemination Analysis Group indicates that

> the study found that few of the existing dissemination activities encourage the kinds of combination of existing networks and capabilities needed to improve educational dissemination in a major way [National Institute for Community Development, 1977, p. i].

This study team went on to identify twelve different operational problems that currently stand in the way of effective educational diffusion. These include failure to delineate target groups properly, failure to use two-way communication, and failure to provide adequate incentives to potential users.

An advisory study committee of the National Academy of Sciences (1974, p. 8), upon completing an investigation of manpower labs supported by the Department of Labor, concluded:

"There is agreement between [Labor Department] and laboratory officials that efforts to promote use of laboratory finds have not been successful." No special effort is required to discover numerous similar published comments concerning the depressing state of utilization of social science research. Our failures in this area are well-known embarrassments to us all.

In the field of business, economic factors constitute the chief spur to diffusion. Distribution and profits are explicitly and functionally intertwined. There is an absence of such an operational incentive in favor of diffusion in the social area. Recent concern on the part of the public for accountability, however, may serve as a stimulus to more active diffusion. In addition, expectations by government and private funding organizations for inclusion of dissemination components in grant proposals may also provide an economic push in that direction. Nevertheless, the development of internalized professional norms, rather than economic levers, in the long run may constitute the main driving force for diffusion in the human service fields.

Social Marketing

Social marketing is a relatively recent concept. It can be identified with one man in particular, Philip Kotler, a professor of marketing at Northwestern University. Its specific origins can be traced to Kotler's article with Levy in 1969, entitled "Broadening the Concept of Marketing" (Kotler & Levy, 1969), in which the authors argue that principles of marketing that have been applied to profit-making organizations can be transferred usefully to nonbusiness settings.

This novel notion was not accepted without contention. A rejoinder was contained in an article by Luck (1969), entitled "Broadening the Concept of Marketing—Too Far." Luck espoused the traditional view restricting marketing to the monetary purchase and sale of goods and services. Nevertheless, in a relatively short period of time social marketing established a firm foothold in the marketing profession. By 1978, Lovelock and Weinberg (1978, pp. 413, 437-438) reported that "public and nonprofit marketing has come of age. . . . No serious controversy remains among academics as to whether or not non-business marketing belongs in the general field of marketing."

Social marketing can best be defined by referring to the writings of Kotler, who is its most avid advocate and substantive conceptualizer. We will base this discussion on his book (Kotler, 1975, 1982) and on several coauthored papers (Kotler & Zaltman, 1971; Fox & Kotler, 1980). The Kotler and Zaltman piece is especially useful for our purposes, and we will draw upon it liberally.

In his 1982 book, Kotler states:

> Social marketing is the design, implementation, and control of programs seeking to increase the acceptability of a social idea or cause in a target group(s). It utilizes concepts of market segregation, consumer research, concept development, communication, facilitation, incentives, and exchange theory to maximize target group response [p. 490].

Marketing is conceived as an exchange process between two or more parties. Communication and distribution are core aspects of such transactions. Basically, marketing entails the conscious analysis and strategic guiding of exchange processes to bring about desired exchange results. A contemporary marketing orientation calls for discerning the needs or wishes of a target audience and then creating and distributing the goods and services necessary to meet these needs. This orientation is contrasted with an earlier "sales orientation," which focused on locating customers for products already in existence and on convincing these individuals to purchase those products. Social marketing (and marketing in general, in this view) is a complex, deliberative process for meeting societal needs, and, "in the hands of its best practitioners, marketing management is applied behavioral science." (Kotler & Zaltman, 1971, p. 5).

Social marketing is analyzed within the framework of basic components of the marketing field originally propounded by McCarthy (1968). These include the four Ps of marketing: product, promotion, place, and price.

With regard to *product,* both business and social organizations must analyze the needs and wants of target audiences and design products and services that are responsive. These must be "packaged" in useful and attractive ways. Kotler and Zaltman (1971, p. 7) state:

> Identical reasoning is required by those who market altruistic causes (e.g., charity giving, blood donation), personal health causes (e.g., nonsmoking, better nutrition), and social betterment causes (e.g., civil rights, improved housing, better environment). In each case, the social marketer must define the change sought, which may be a change of values, beliefs, affects, behavior, or some mixture. He must meaningfully segment the target markets. He must design social products for each market which are "buyable," and which instrumentally serve the social cause. In some social causes, the most difficult problem will be to innovate appropriate products, in other cases it will be to motivate purchase.

The view is expressed that packaging is more difficult in the social field because of the less tangible quality of the product. The difference in the two areas is in concreteness and ease of execution, rather than in the fundamental character of the process.

With regard to *promotion,* communication and persuasion are at the heart of the matter. One must present the product in a way that seems acceptable and desirable to potential users. Typical marketing techniques include advertising, personal selling, publicity, and sales promotion. The marketer must make informed decisions about which of these to employ and in what type of mix, given the characteristics of the target audience and the resources available for reaching it.

The question of advertising style or tone arises in this connection. Kotler and Zaltman (1971, p. 8) have these comments:

> Many persons mistakenly assume that marketing means hard selling. This is only a particular style of marketing, and it has its critics both inside and outside the profession. There are many firms that market their products with taste and sensitivity: examples include Xerox, Container Corporation, and Hallmark.

Nevertheless, much commercial marketing is intrusive, crass, and, indeed, lacking in taste. A constructive transfer of marketing methods to the social field would screen out and discard such aspects. Otherwise the exercise could be analogous to spreading a plague deliberately from one place to another. These unique social and ethical aspects of social marketing are discussed by several authors and from varying perspectives in the Lazer and Kelley (1973) compilation on social marketing. Kotler (1982, p. xiv) is especially sensitive to the problem:

> The transposition of a conceptual system from one domain (the profit sector) to another (the nonprofit sector) poses a number of challenges that call for creative translation. The concepts of product, price, promotion, and distribution, which are employed by profit-sector marketers, have to be redefined for maximum relevance to all organizations. The concepts of markets and exchange processes must be generalized. The concept of profit maximization must be translated into benefit-cost maximization so that marketing models can be applied fruitfully in the nonprofit sector.

This accepted, however, style or personal aesthetics must be weighed carefully against results in attaining a worthy social goal, such as funds for cancer research or better mental health services.

Place refers to contact points where exchange relationships actually occur. Stated another way, there must be provision of adequate channels for distribution and for response. In business, a retail store is the most typical locale in which marketing occurs. Such established institutions and mechanisms are lacking in the social field. Thus careful attention must be given to offering action outlets. For example, in a drive to urge people to stop the smoking habit, individuals must know where and how to sign up for instruction. An environmental protection campaign might indicate how one can sign a petition to preserve national parks. As Kotler and Zaltman (1971, p. 9) observe:

> Thus, place means arranging for accessible outlets which permit the translation of motivations into actions. Planning in this area entails

selecting or developing appropriate outlets, deciding on their number, average size, and locations, and giving them proper motivation
to perform their part of the job.

The final marketing consideration is *price*. In commercial
marketing this is a central issue since profit is a propelling force.
Price may be a factor in some nonbusiness marketing. The
diffusing agency in some instances may be concerned about
recovering basic costs of providing a product or service. But
there are other than monetary costs to a potential user that
must go into the social marketing plan: energy costs, psychic
costs, opportunity costs. The user must be convinced that the
risk, inconvenience, or effort involved in trying a new approach
is compelling compared to continuing with the "tried and true"
or doing nothing. The social marketer must understand that the
target user will engage in an informal cost-benefit analysis in
making a decision about adoption, and the marketer's task is to
structure the exchange in a way that reduces the many intan-
gible costs and highlights the benefits to the user. As Kotler and
Zaltman (1971, p. 10) state:

> Social marketing requires that careful thought be given to the
> manner in which manageable, desirable, gratifying and convenient
> solutions to a perceived need or problem are presented to its poten-
> tial buyers.

Fox and Kotler (1980) have identified what they term "elements of social marketing." We touched upon two of these
earlier. One is sophisticated social research in order to understand the market and discover effective ways of reaching and
motivating it. The second is the use of incentives. The social
marketing specialist, according to Fox and Kotler, should be
expert in knowing what kinds of incentives stimulate different
kinds of behaviors and change activities.[2] This requires knowledge and methods to maintain new behavior in addition to
methods of bringing about initial adoption. These authors also
delineate a number of special functions of social marketing
(related to conditions when it is appropriate): providing infor-

mation when new practices need to be disseminated (convincing people in developing countries to boil their water and cover up the water supply); providing countermarketing to offset negative advertising (discouraging consumption of alcohol and highly refined foods that contribute to heart disease and overweight); and activating people to take realistic steps in directions they already know are beneficial (such as getting more exercise or spending more time with the family).

Kotler (1975) has presented a conceptual schema that captures both a range of key components and the processual flow of activity in social marketing (Figure 2.2). It offers a useful general frame of reference for the analysis of social marketing.

Some variations in definition have appeared among different writers on the subject. Fox and Kotler (1980), for example, distinguish between social marketing and nonprofit organization marketing. In their view, the term "social marketing" should be restricted to activities geared to promoting social causes, disseminating social ideas, and pursuing public issues. "Nonprofit marketing," on the other hand, they see as dealing with ways by which a wide range of different nonbusiness organizations communicate with the various markets. The Right to Life movement, in disseminating antiabortion information, would be engaged, in this formulation, in social marketing; the United Way, in asking for contributions from different publics for its annual campaign, would be carrying out nonprofit marketing. The distinction seems a fine one to us and is difficult to sustain. Lovelock and Weinberg (1978) use "public and nonprofit marketing" as a single term to cut across both areas without distinction. The specific study we will describe combines elements of the twofold distinction of Fox and Kotler.

The definitional issue is confounded by other authors who extend the concept beyond what appears to be reasonable bounds. Lazer and Kelley (1973), for example, include articles in their edited collection that deal with the social responsibilities and social impacts of marketing. Here, one is dealing with social spillovers of traditional, business-oriented marketing. For our purposes, we will exclude such considerations from our

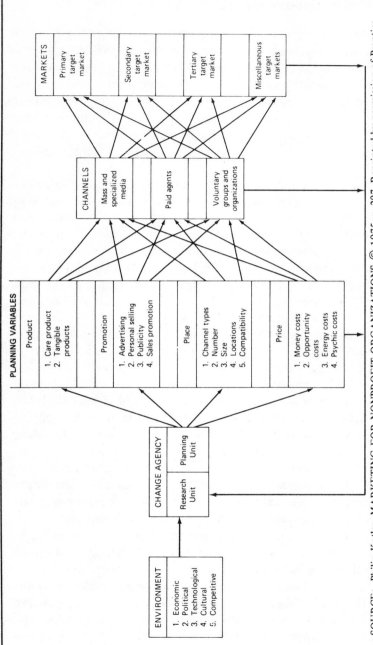

SOURCE: Philip Kotler, MARKETING FOR NONPROFIT ORGANIZATIONS, © 1975, p. 297. Reprinted by permission of Prentice-Hall, Inc., Englewood Cliffs, N.J.

Figure 2.2: Kotler's Conceptual Scheme of Marketing

definition. We will, however, employ "social marketing" as an overarching or generic term for systematic marketing in the social field. It will include social cause marketing, nonprofit organization marketing, social advertising, social communication, and the like. A newer general treatment is offered by Fine (1982), while the Graduate School of Business Administration at the University of Michigan has recently begun sponsoring a new professional publication, the *Journal of Marketing and Public Policy.*

Moving from a general to a more concrete level of discussion, social marketing activities have been reported in a wide range of different fields of endeavor. Some of these—and this listing does not begin to be exhaustive—include *health care* (Mushkin, 1974; Somers, 1976; Richard et al., 1976); *higher education* (Kotler & Dubois, 1974; Cook et al., 1977; Leister & MacLachlan, 1976); *environmental protection* (Zikmund & Stanton, 1971; Margulies, 1970); *energy conservation* (Montgomery & Leonard-Barton, 1977; Phillips & Nelson, 1976; Russo, 1977); *the arts* (Morison & Fliehr, 1968; Weinberg, 1977; Loczniak & Murphy, 1977); and *public transportation* (Schneider, 1965; Gilbert & Foerster, 1977; Vanier & Wotruba, 1977). There has been a dearth of applications in mental health or social services, although a few isolated examples can be cited (Chisnall, 1979; Simon & McArdle, 1975). For detailed illustrations of applications in a multiplicity of fields, a good source is Gaedeke (1977).

Though it is possible to identify common elements of marketing in the business and social worlds, this does not imply that methods are by any means identical in the two spheres. Certainly, we must consider the possibility of important ethical and stylistic differences in the way marketing is conducted in the two areas. Our earlier comment on the character of advertising and packaging applies here. In addition, there is an empirical lack of goodness of fit and significant obstacles in transferring this technology from the business to the social realm. Fox and Kotler (1980) identify a number of these hurdles. The social market is harder to analyze because there is an absence of

quality data about consumers. It is more difficult to use segmenting procedures because there is frequently pressure to serve
the entire market, rather than a portion of it, simultaneously
and equitably. The pricing variable is less malleable. Distribution channels are unavailable or difficult to control. Social
organizations are frequently unsophisticated with regard to
management and marketing know-how. Finally, evaluating the
results of marketing endeavors is problematic—the proverbial
"bottom line" is missing. Fox and Kotler acknowledge that
during this early state of development there will be problems in
employing social marketing for "promoting beneficial social
change in an effective manner." At the same time they see
prospects as promising:

> Social marketing specialists, combining business marketing skills
> with additional training in the social sciences, will be working on a
> wider range of social causes with increasing sophistication. Advances
> in conceptualizing social marketing problems and evaluating the
> impacts of social marketing programs will further enhance their
> effectiveness [Fox & Kotler, 1980, p. 32].

The work presented in this book may be viewed as part of that
effort.

Diffusion in the Social Sciences

We do not mean to imply, nor would Kotler so argue, that
the transfer of knowledge is a one-way affair—from business
marketing techniques to the social field. Indeed, from one
perspective, at least, it is certainly arguable that the entire field
of marketing is itself a social science discipline, rooted firmly in
the academic traditions of psychology and social psychology. In
addition, King (1966) describes the carryover of research and
theory from the diffusion literature of the social sciences to the
field of marketing. In King's (1966, p. 684) view, the "diffusion
research tradition can make a unique contribution to more
efficient new product marketing and to understanding the dif-

fusion process in the mass consumer market context." Clearly, then, activities converge in these seemly disparate fields.

Of the various phases of R&D (retrieval, codification and synthesis, conversion and design, development and diffusion), perhaps the most substantial accumulation of theory development and research (as far as the social sciences are concerned) is in the area of diffusion. This considerable outpouring of research has been gathered and synthesized in major volumes of scholars such as Rogers and Shoemaker (1971), Glaser (1967), Zaltman et al. (1973), Havelock (1968), and Rothman (1974). Well-authenticated generalizations have been formulated with regard to factors such as stages in the innovation process, different innovation roles and actors, characteristics of innovators, and the place of "opinion leaders" in the two-step flow of communication. More recent developments have included the delineation of organizational variables associated with the adoption of innovations, and of collective and authority decisions as part of the diffusion process. Rogers and Shoemaker (1971) indicate that the diffusion tradition in the social sciences has been fed by such diverse fields as rural sociology and agricultural extension, anthropology, education, medical sociology, and communications—and, of course, marketing.

One is led to conclude that the knowledge component of diffusion is under much more control in the social fields than is its applied expression. Some few, sustained, action-research diffusion undertakings, however, have been ventured and reported upon. One such study by Fairweather and his associates (1974) has attracted wide professional notice. The study team engaged in a protracted campaign to diffuse a new mental health service program, the "lodge model," that consists of a largely self-directed halfway house for patients discharged from mental hospitals. The lodge concept orginally emerged from a form of development effort called "experimental social innovation." This effort involved the collaboration of researchers and mental health practitioners. When the "demonstration" lodge failed to be adopted, even by the hospital that cooperated in the experiment, the Fairweather group decided to initiate a national dissemination effort among mental health hospitals. Three different strategies of dissemination were employed: a brochure, workshops, and on-site demonstrations. It was found that the demonstration modality was most effective in stimulating adoption, and that other factors also contributed to utilization, such as action consultation and user participation.

Another example is the vocational rehabilitation project by Glaser (1967) to obtain widespread use of a new program for placing mentally retarded young men into gainful employment. This program, based on the work of the Tacoma Goodwill Industries, was disseminated through three distinct diffusion strategies as well: a booklet, a conference at the demonstration site, and a consultation visit to potential adopter sites. It was found that the combination of booklet and demonstration conference had the greatest diffusion payoff.

In a later experience, Glaser and Ross (1971) undertook the dissemination of a new mental health technique called "saturation group therapy," a prolonged series of weekend group treatment sessions. Varied diffusion strategies were employed, including a descriptive pamphlet, a consultation visit to the user site, a visit by users to the central demonstration site, and a consultation visit to the user site following the demonstration observation. These investigators found that an insignificant number of adoptions or adaptations of the program were made. They attributed this to the nature of the innovation itself. They indicated that careful screening must take place regarding innovations to be disseminated to ensure that these have relevance for the target organizations and that they can be adopted readily within the user's normal environment. The authors conclude that the character of the product itself and the means of diffusing it are critical considerations in bringing about utilization. This is consistent with our view.

Here, then, are three different examples of attempts to channel a developed product or service to "consumers" who will use it. Had we been describing events in the commercial sphere, we would say, simply, here are three marketing efforts. These three particular efforts, however, were directed to the channeling of three social problem-solving, application concepts. These, then, were efforts at social marketing.

The lesson of these and similar efforts is that utilization depends on a "product advocacy" or "campaign" outlook, carefully articulated with social marketing methods and procedures conducive to user adoption. In other words, the same attention, drive, and competency that goes into formulating a research study or into doing development work must also be given to the design of a plan of diffusion.

Broader and firmer conclusions concerning the processes and effects of diffusion are available in the works of Rogers and others described earlier, who generally based their studies on the diffusion efforts of *others*. Because of a more limited experience, action-research or field experiment diffusion studies have offered fewer generalizations to this point, but they may in the long run provide a particularly rich source of knowledge concerning the phenomenon.

Few human service professionals would argue that the present tools of our trade are adequate to deal with the huge social and personal problems that come before struggling practitioners and administrators in human service agencies. Even when effective new technologies do come into being, they tend to diffuse through the professional infrastructure in a slow and halting manner. The lag between the creation of an innovative idea or technique and its widespread application may involve years, even decades.

There are, of course, understandable reasons for this. Making a change requires extra thought, effort, and a spirit of venturesomeness that not everyone possesses. While there may be enormous benefits inherent in adopting strategies, or analogues of strategies, from different disciplines and professions, there are also enormous dangers. With specific reference to social marketing, for example, we take unto ourselves those same troubling issues and concerns that confront present-day marketers. In the matter of marketing ethics, for example, there are vexatious problems relating to the market research function, with its implications for the invasion of personal privacy and problems related to product management, distribution strategies, and the pricing of the products developed from social R&D. There is a very special ethical problem involved in promoting the products of social R&D: Should a tool or program or service designed to enhance the employability of the hardcore unemployed, for example, be hawked like soap?

Our own R&D efforts in the Community Intervention Project involved meeting and dealing with a two-level problem of acceptance. First, we were developing a methodology for the invention of new, need-specific practice strategies. This methodology, because of its antecedents in the business and industrial worlds, was—and quite properly should have been—suspect with respect to its relevance to social problem solving. Second, having demonstrated with reasonable success the utility of social R&D by developing new and useful practice tools, it was necessary to determine effective ways of disseminating these in a timely fashion to those who could use them to advantage in problem solving. This involved developing and executing a dissemination plan (that is, a social marketing effort) that would place a product of our R&D effort (our intervention strategies handbook) in the hands of the appropriate "consumers" (that is, mental health practitioners—our market) who might benefit from the product.

Two Studies in Social Marketing

All of this brings us to the rationale for this volume. In the pages that follow we shall present two exploratory ventures in social marketing. The greatest part of the body of diffusion literature reports on efforts to understand the natural processes of diffusion that take place as one might observe how a substance ingested into the human body is distributed by the vascular system. Certainly, this is a concern for diffusion investigation. There is a component of planned manipulation of channels and techniques in social marketing, however, that is not generally dealt with in the diffusion studies that have been reported. Our field experiments, in contrast, were action-research endeavors in which data gathering and social change objectives were both present and controlled by the research team.

Traditionally, commercial diffusion programs have included a marketing research component that aims at assessing the extent of consumer interests, desires, and responses. Tinnesand (1975) correctly points out that there are a variety of different types of marketing research that may be related to different functions and stages of the R&D process. One way of making distinctions is to discriminate between market research or market analysis and test marketing. Market research is said by Tinnesand to refer to "market environment of the organization." This type of research takes place at the inception stage of R&D. It signals whether a need exists for a given potential R&D product, and it indicates whether a particular R&D endeavor should be initiated at all. It asks whether a pool of potential users is standing by to engage a given output. Test marketing, on the other hand, takes place on the opposite end of the R&D continuum, after a product has been brought to full development. It is a form of operations research that seeks to discover where potential users are located, their characteristics, and through what means they might best be reached. The studies that will be described in this book may best be viewed as a form of test marketing.

The specific product developed from our social R&D activities was a handbook for human service professionals working in community mental health and family service agencies. The handbook was a procedural guide, designed to aid professionals in gaining acceptance of innovative programs or services in the community and attaining increased participation in organizations, voluntary associations, or task groups. The application concepts offered to the practitioner had been field tested and subjected to various investigations to determine the most acceptable form of presentation and packaging; the final handbook product, itself, was test marketed to determine its likelihood of acceptance by the general market: community mental health and family service agency practitioners. There remained for us to determine some effective method of reaching our market.

The handbook was focused on assisting mental health practitioners in carrying out community- and organizational-level interventions. Many professionals in the field are highly skilled and informed with regard to interpersonal aspects of their work. Many, however, lack formal training and a working sophistication in dealing with the social systems impinging on their clients or the agencies in which they function. We felt it would be a worthwhile goal to enhance the skills of practitioners in these less familiar areas. In keeping with a fundamental marketing approach, product development to meet social needs was a prelude to promotional activity.

The need for a marketing approach is supplied by Mechanic (1980, pp. 178, 183), who indicates that innovative mental health ideas "face considerable difficulty in becoming widely accepted and used. . . . It . . . requires the leadership to attract people to new jobs and tasks and to stimulate their motivation and commitment."

The particular contribution of the handbook is in the area of broad prevention. It equips mental health practitioners with skills related to areas such as (1) outreach services, (2) family life education, (3) consultation to primary care-giving institutions, (4) enhancing the effects of natural care givers in informal care-giving situations, (5) elimination of stressful social conditions that place strains on family functioning, and (6) providing opportunities for meaningful community participation and problem solving. While the community mental health literature vigorously promotes such activities, personnel often lack the skills or orientation to implement them.

As we mentioned earlier, diffusion methods have been discussed by Rogers and Shoemaker (1971), Zaltman et al. (1973), and others, and there are a multitude of approaches that might be taken. These can be conceptualized in two broad categories: "high intensity" (personal contact approaches) and "low intensity" (mass communication, impersonal approaches). High-intensity approaches, using high-involvement media, offer a greater degree of personal interaction, immediate feedback, and focused expertise. Such approaches require a large investment in staff time and financial resources, however, and ordinarily cover a smaller number of potential users. Low-intensity techniques, in comparison, employing low-involvement media, reach larger numbers of people and ordinarily require fewer resources per contact. Their drawback is that they allow less initiative and flexibility in influencing potential users. Litwak (1959) provides us with a cogent discussion of these theoretical perspectives.

As high-intensity approaches are considerably more expensive in terms of human resources, time, travel, facilities, and other costs, not all agencies have the resources to engage in this type of diffusion. Further, such procedures ordinarily sacrifice communication with a larger pool of potential users. Utilizing this larger pool might well result in greater aggregate utilization. In the event that what is communicated is simple or that the audience is favorable or highly motivated, a low-intensity approach might be preferred.

These concepts and issues are consistent with thinking in the marketing field. Marketing promotional methods, for example, are ordinarily assumed to include advertising (low intensity) and personal selling (high intensity), and such supplementary methods as consumer promotions (contests and the like), shows and exhibits, displays and demonstrations, public relations, and publicity (Rewoldt et al., 1973; Boone & Kurtz, 1977). Rewoldt et al. (1973) summarize writings on the relative advantages of advertising and personal selling approaches. Advertising is said to be the preferred mode when the company "is operating with a favorable *primarily demand trend*" (p. 483; emphasis in original). On the other hand, personal selling is advisable "when the product has features which require explanation or demonstration" (p. 483), including high cost, an infrequent purchase, or a trade-in situation. These authors and others (Borden, 1967; DeLozier, 1976) speak as well to considerations of a "promotional mix" (a direct mailing, plus a phone call, and then a knock on the door), wherein combinations of approaches are employed conjointly with varying relative emphases. We shall have more to say about this later.

In most discussions of diffusion in the human services literature there is an implication that high-intensity approaches are more effective in promoting utilization of new practice tools. We have been able to discover little human services or social science research that deals generally and comparatively with effectiveness of mass communication versus interpersonal modes of diffusion. Some studies, such as one by Glaser (1967), however, do indicate that increased "increments of communication," involving progressively more interpersonal intensity, were associated with a higher rate of use of an innovative practice in the field of rehabilitation services.

From a pragmatic point of view, human service agencies will continue to use both approaches, based on available resources, ideological preferences, and complexity of innovations. Accepting this as an organizational "fact of life" in the human services field, the Community Intervention Project employed alternative diffusion procedures within both high- and low-intensity approaches.

We asked: "Given that you are able to, or prefer to, use a mass communication approach or a personal contact approach in diffusing a new practice technique, what are more effective ways within each type of approach to achieve a high adoption rate among target practitioners?" We wished, also, to assess cost-effective variation between the two basic approaches.

The first of the social marketing studies on which we shall report is the "low-intensity" study, which used an impersonal, mass communication approach through direct mailings to mental health agencies. We examined the effects of different written "reference group appeals" to the target professional market and different points of entry into the agency system. The reference appeals took account of differential identification with one's profession, with one's employing agency, and with the clientele and community being served. The general direction of inquiry in the study is suggested by Kotler (1982, pp. 489-490):

> The adoption of an idea, like the adoption of any product, requires a deep understanding of the needs, perceptions, preferences, reference groups, and behavioral patterns of the target audience, and the tailoring of messages, media, costs, and facilities to maximize the ease of adopting the idea. We use the term *social marketing* to cover

these tasks. We believe that social marketing provides an effective conceptual system for thinking through the problems of bringing about changes in the ideas or practices of a target public.

Not all of this could or would be undertaken in one study. A start, however, could be made.

Following that discussion, we will turn to the second social marketing experiment, the "high-intensity" study, which focused on effects of personal contact by a diffusion agent within an agency. Particular attention was paid to the type of diffusion agent that is most effective in marketing innovative professional practices (internal versus external agent; authority versus peer). Personal contact was largely through the medium of a workshop training event.

While the outcome of this book is primarily scientific or knowledge producing, it also has strong implications for conducting action programs in staff development and training for human service professionals. It will suggest some means for disseminating training materials or innovative practices and some means for structuring training workshops.

Conclusion

In 1789, Benjamin Franklin wrote to M. Leroy that there is nothing certain in this world but death and taxes. Now, with tax rebellions on every hand and the developing science of cryogenics, even these "certainties" may be in doubt. In our work we assumed one clear certainty: If solid linkage is not forged between research and practice, between innovations and potential users in the human services, human needs will continue to be met in a halting and unsatisfactory fashion.

In the CIP we have written extensively on the various aspects of the research utilization model that guided our activities: social problem identification, information retrieval related to the identified problem, the development of consensus generalizations based upon existing research, the conversion of such generalizations into applied forms that constitute guides to action, the testing of those guides, and the packaging of tested intervention procedures in a form useful to practitioners. In this presentation we direct ourselves substantially for the first time to the last step in research utilization: social marketing in the human services. The deficiencies in our work will be readily apparent. In defense we plead ignorance. We were not altogether sure where to begin, or, once begun, where our journey would take us. If nothing else, the two small efforts reported here should at least provide a more readily identifiable stepping-off place for others who wish to explore the still indistinct terrain of human services social marketing.

Notes

1. Portions of the sections that follow are adapted from Chapter 10 in Jack Rothman, *Social R&D: Research and Development in the Human Services,* ©1980. Reprinted by permission of Prentice-Hall, Inc., Englewood Cliffs, NJ.

2. Knowing what kinds of incentives or rewards stimulate different kinds of behaviors and change activities is a far more complicated proposition than it first appears. It necessitates studying the target market carefully in order to determine what has been rewarding in the past. One of the most common mistakes of marketers is to make assumptions about what constitutes incentives or rewards for those whose behaviors one seeks to modify. Behavioral psychologists learned long ago that if one wants to train a pigeon to perform a task, the pigeon must be rewarded. However, it is the pigeon, not the trainer, who makes the determination of what is rewarding. It is the target market, not the marketer, that determines what rewards or incentives will stimulate different kinds of behaviors and change activities.

References

Ansoff, H. I. Evaluation of applied research in a business firm. In J. R. Bright (Ed.), *Technological planning on the corporate level, proceedings of a conference sponsored by the Associates of the Harvard Business School, September 8 & 9.* Cambridge, MA: Harvard Business School, 1961.

Boone, L. & Kurtz, D. L. *Foundations of marketing.* Hinsdale, IL: Dryden, 1977.

Borden, N. H. *The concept of the marketing mix.* In P. R. Cateora & L. Richardson (Eds.), *Readings in marketing: The qualitative and quantitative areas.* New York: Meredith, 1967.

Chisnall, P. M. The contribution of marketing research to health and welfare programs. *Administration in Social Work,* 1979, 3(3), 337-348.

Cook, R. W., Krampf, R. F. & Shimp, T. A. A nonmetric multidimensional approach to the marketing of higher educational institutions. *Proceedings of the 9th Annual Conference, American Institute for Decision Sciences,* 1977.

DeLozier, M. W. *The marketing communications process.* New York: McGraw-Hill, 1976.

Fairweather, G. W., Sanders, D. H., & Tornatzky, L. G. *Creating change in mental health organizations.* New York: Pergamon, 1974.

Fine, S. *Marketing of ideas and social issues.* New York: Praeger, 1982.

Fox, F. A., & Kotler, P. The marketing of social causes: The first ten years. *Journal of Marketing,* 1980, 44 (Fall), 24-33.

Gaedeke, R. M. (Ed.). *Marketing in private and public nonprofit organizations: Perspectives and illustrations.* Santa Monica, CA: Goodyear, 1977.

Gilbert, G., & Foerster, J. The importance of attitudes in the decision to use mass transit. *Transportation,* 1977, 6, 321-332.

Glaser, E. M. *Utilization of applicable research and demonstration results.* Final report to Vocational Rehabilitation Administration, Department of Health, Education and Welfare, March 1967.

Glaser, E. M., & Ross, H. L. *Increasing the utilization of applied research results* (final report to the National Institute of Mental Health). Los Angeles: Human Interaction Institute, 1971.

Guba, E. G. Development, diffusion and evaluation. In T. L. Eiddell & J. M. Kitchel (Eds.), *Knowledge production and utilization.* Columbus, OH: University Council for Educational Administration, and Eugene: Center for the Advanced Study of Educational Administration, University of Oregon, 1968.

Havelock, R. G. Dissemination and translation roles. In T. L. Eiddell & J. M. Kitchel (Eds.), *Knowledge production and utilization.* Columbus, OH: University Council for Educational Administration, and Eugene: Center for the Advanced Study of Educational Administration, University of Oregon, 1968.

King, C. W. Adoption and diffusion research in marketing: An overview. Reprinted from *Science, Technology and Marketing,* reprint series 188. Lafayette, IN: Herman C. Krannert Graduate School of Industrial Administration, Purdue University, 1966.

Kotler, P. *Marketing for nonprofit organizations.* Englewood Cliffs, NJ: Prentice-Hall, 1975.

Kotler, P. *Marketing for nonprofit organizations* (2nd ed.). Englewood Cliffs, NJ: Prentice-Hall, 1982.

Kotler, P., & Dubois, B. Educational problems and marketing. In J. N. Sheth & P. L. Wright (Eds.), *Marketing analysis for societal problems.* Urbana: University of Illinois, 1974.

Kotler, P., & Levy, S. J. Broadening the concept of marketing. *Journal of Marketing,* 1969, 33(1), 10-15.

Kotler, P., & Zaltman, G. Social marketing: An approach to planned social change. *Journal of Marketing,* 1971, 35(3), 3-12.

Lazer, W., & Kelley, E. J. *Social marketing: Perspectives and viewpoints.* Homewood, IL: Irwin, 1973.

Leister, D. V., & MacLachlan, D. L. Assessing the community college transfer market: A metamarketing application. *Journal of Higher Education,* 1976, 47, 661-680.

Litwak, E. Some policy implications in communications theory with emphasis on group factors. In Council on Social Work Education, *Education for social work, proceedings of the seventh annual program meeting.* New York: Council on Social Work Education, 1959.

Loczniak, G. R., & Murphy, P. E. Planning and control for performing arts marketing. In B. E. Greenberg & D. E. Bellenger (Eds.), *1977 educators' proceedings.* Chicago: American Marketing Association, 1977.

Lovelock, C. H., & Weinberg, C. B. Public and nonprofit marketing comes of age. In G. Zaltman & T. V. Bonoma (Eds.), *Review of marketing, 1978.* Pittsburgh: American Marketing Association, Marketing Science Institute, and University of Pittsburgh, 1978.

Luck, D. J. Broadening the concept of marketing—Too far. *Journal of Marketing,* 1969, 33(2), 53-55.

McCarthy, E. J. *Basic marketing: A managerial approach* (3rd ed.). Homewood, IL: Irwin, 1968.

Margulies, W. P. Glass, paper makers tackle our packaging pollution woes. *Advertising Age,* September 21, 1970, p. 43.

Mechanic, D. *Mental health and social policy* (2nd ed.). Englewood Cliffs, NJ: Prentice-Hall, 1980.

Montgomery, D. B., & Leonard-Barton, D. *Toward strategies for marketing home energy conservation* (Research Paper 372). Stanford, CA: Stanford University Graduate School of Business, 1977.

Morison, B. G., & Fliehr, K. *In search of an audience.* New York: Pittman, 1968.

Mushkin, S. (Ed.). *Consumer incentives for health care.* New York: Prodist, 1974.

National Academy of Sciences, National Research Council. *The experimental manpower laboratory as an R&D capability.* Washington, DC: Author, 1974.

National Institute for Community Development, Inc. *Dissemination in relation to elementary and secondary education: Final report of the Dissemination Analysis Group to the Dissemination Policy Council.* Washington, DC: Author, 1977.

Phillips, N., & Nelson, E. Energy savings in private households—An integrated research programme. *Journal of the Market Research Society,* 1976, 18, 180-200.

Radnor, M., et al. *Agency/field relationships in the educational R/D&I system: A policy analysis for the national institute of education.* Evanston, IL: Center for the Interdisciplinary Study of Science and Technology, Northwestern University, 1976.

Rewoldt, S. H., Scott, J. D. & Warshaw, M. R. *Introduction to marketing management: Text and cases.* Homewood, IL: Irwin, 1973. (See also 1981 edition.)

Richard, L., Becherer, R., & George, W. R. The development of marketing management technology in a health care setting: The health maintenance organization experience. In K. L. Bernhardt (Ed.), *1976 educators' proceedings.* Chicago: American Marketing Association, 1976.

Rogers, E. M., & Shoemaker, F. F. *Communication of innovations* (2nd ed.). New York: Macmillan, 1971.

Rothman, J. *Planning and organizing for social change: Action guidelines from social science research.* New York: Columbia University Press, 1974.

Rothman, J. *Social R&D: Research and development in the human services.* Englewood Cliffs, NJ: Prentice-Hall, 1980.

Rothman, J., Erlich, J. L., & Teresa, J. G. *Promoting innovation and change in organizations and communities: A planning manual.* New York: John Wiley, 1976.

Rothman, J., Erlich, J. L., & Teresa, J. G. *Changing organizations and community programs.* Beverly Hills, CA: Sage, 1981.

Rothman, J., Teresa, J. G., & Erlich, J. L. *Developing effective strategies of social intervention: a research and development methodology* (PB-272454 TR-1-RD). Springfield, VA: National Technical Information Service, 1977.

Rothman, J., Teresa, J. G., & Erlich, J. L. *Fostering participation and innovation: Handbook for human service professionals.* Itasca, IL: Peacock, 1978.

Russo, E. A proposal to increase energy conservation through provision of consumer and cost information to consumers. In E. B. Greenberg & D. E. Bellenger (Eds.), *1977 educators' proceedings.* Chicago: American Marketing Association, 1977.

Schneider, L. M. *Marketing urban mass transit—A comparative study of management strategies.* Boston: Division of Research, Harvard Graduate School of Business Administration, 1965.

Simon, J. L., & McArdle, P. Marketing EPSTD to clients. *Social and Rehabilitation Service,* HEW, June 1975.

Somers, A. R. (Ed.). *Promoting health: Consumer education and national policy.* Germantown, MD: Aspen Systems Corporation, 1976.

Tinnesand, B. The importance of market research and intelligence in the innovation process. In K. Holt (Ed.), *Product innovation: Models and methods.* Trodheim, Norway: Norwegian Institute of Technology, Section of Industrial Management, 1975.

Tornatzky, L. G., & Fairweather, G. *The role of experimental research in a social change process.* Paper presented at the annual meeting of the American Psychological Association, Washington, D.C., September 1976.

University of Michigan, Division of Research Development and Administration. The Community Intervention Project. *Research News,* 1977, 27(6), 17-22.

Vanier, D., & Wotruba, T. R. Mass transit: Devising a research based marketing plan. *Transportation Research,* 1977, 11, 245-253.

Weinberg, C. B. Building a marketing plan for the performing arts. *Association of College, University and Community Arts Administrators Bulletin,* May 1977.

Zaltman, G., Duncan, R., & Holbek, J. *Innovations and organizations.* New York: John Wiley, 1973.

Zikmund, W. G., & Stanton, W. J. Recycling solid wastes: A channels-of-distribution problem. *Journal of Marketing,* 1971, 35(July), 34-39.

PART II

A MASS COMMUNICATIONS APPROACH TO SOCIAL MARKETING

CHAPTER 3

ISSUES IN MASS COMMUNICATIONS SOCIAL MARKETING

A Brief Look Forward

In this chapter we discuss a mass communications approach involving direct mailings to agencies as a means of marketing innovative professional practices. We examine first the issue of reference group appeals as related to professional identification, suggesting three different types of appeals: Bureaucratic, Professional, and Community/Client. We hypothesize which of the appeals will be most effective in stimulating use of innovative practices in the two service systems we were targeting: community mental health centers and family service agencies. In addition, we indicate tentative hypotheses concerning which appeals will be most effective, depending on personal characteristics of professionals such as age, sex, years of experience, and educational level. We likewise suggest hypothesized reactions to different appeals based on organizational structural variables such as the size of the agency, presence of minority staff, and proportion of non-human service auxiliary staff in the organization.

A second major area of our discussion focuses on the optimal point of entry into the agency when undertaking direct mailings; that is, whether it is better to go through the executive at the top or through different types of middle-echelon personnel. Based on an analysis of the character of human service organizations, we offer a somewhat surprising hypothesis regarding this. This discussion of theoretical perspectives and specific hypotheses is intended to lead into a discussion of the method of investigation, presented in the next chapter.

Preliminary Considerations

Low-intensity social marketing, as we use the term here and throughout this presentation, can be seen as roughly analogous to the process in which a manufacturer would engage in the mass advertising of a new product. The research and development process that gave rise to the product has made a reasonable determination that the product is reliable and useful; however, that is not a necessary and sufficient condition to guarantee the product's use. The intended user must become aware of the product and must be persuaded to adopt, use, or buy it.

Advertising, of course, may mean different things to different people—even different things to the same people at different times. For some it is the linchpin of our free enterprise market system. For others it represents an irritating intrusion into their lives. Various pay-television services cite the absence of advertising as a reason for purchasing the service. Free-television broadcasters cite the presence of advertising as the factor that makes their service possible. Almost no one maintains a view of advertising that is relatively free of positive or negative affect.

Regardless of one's personal views, it is clear that advertising in some form is an essential element in marketing, and, therefore, an essential element in social marketing. Thus it would be well to establish a common ground in our understanding of precisely what we are talking about when we speak of "advertising." We turn to Kotler (1982, p. 356) for our definition:

Advertising consists of *nonpersonal forms of communication conducted through paid media under clear sponsorship.* It involves such varied media as *magazines* and *newspapers; radio* and *television; outdoor* (such as posters, signs, skywriting); *novelties* (matchbooks, calendars); *cards* (car, bus); *catalogs; directories* and *references; programs* and *menus; circulars;* and *direct mail.* It can be carried out for such diverse purposes as long-term buildup of the organization's name (institutional advertising), long-term buildup of a particular product (product advertising) or brand (brand advertising), information dissemination about a sale, service, or event (classified advertising), announcement of a special sale (sales advertising), and so on [emphasis in original].

The social marketer's task is, at the present time, less defined and more complex than that of the more established commercial marketer. The social marketer does not advocate and does not defend the adoption of current commercial practices as such. Rather, he or she sets out to determine what it is in the processes employed by other disciplines, professions, vocations, and fields of human activity that can be brought to bear effectively and ethically on meeting the needs of clients and facilitating the practices of professionals in the human service fields. There then follows a process of extrapolation, modification, or reinvention in order to fit what is useful to a setting, emphasizing service rather than monetary gain.

In our marketing effort we recognized that those in the human services have severe difficulty in getting innovative problem-solving tools widely recognized and used. Our solution to that problem, then, was to discover the mechanisms that are effectively employed in solving that problem, to introduce dynamics of demonstrated effectiveness elsewhere into the social diffusion process, and to understand thoroughly how those dynamics work in this new setting. Thus we were concerned both with *how* the social advertising (low-intensity) methodology works and whether it works. We endeavored to formulate testable hypotheses in this marketing experiment. These will be discussed at length in this chapter. Our fundamental purpose was to maximize the value of the data our effort developed, in the hope that they would provide new knowledge that would permit insightful leaps across the marketing process. It is important to keep in mind, as we examine the details and results of our procedures, that a major concern and primary interest was to examine the social marketing methodology *in process* and to experiment with some of the tools and techniques of the traditional marketing and advertising fields. With this in mind, we turn now to our procedures for studying that methodology in the low-intensity study.

Two Communication Approaches to a Target Market

For our purposes, two issues were selected as being of importance in dealing with mass dissemination. The first issue was the nature of the message or *appeal* that should be contained in our "new product" message; that is, which of the various reference groups with which a professional identifies should be invoked as a source of legitimation or exhortation. We shall call this message aspect "reference group appeal."

The second issue concerned the *point of entry* into the system (or target market) we desired to reach. We were particularly concerned with the matter of what level in human service organizations should be specifically selected to receive our "new product" message; that is, we needed to ascertain the most effective point in the organization for breaching the system boundary.

Westley (1971, p. 737) raises questions concerning change and the diffusion of innovative material:

> If we are to introduce change in something, we must communicate to someone. What shall we communicate, to whom, and through what channels?

Ward et al. (1974, p. 139) indicate that there is a deficit of knowledge on this question:

> Further research [on communications channels] appears called for, with particular attention to such underlying variables as differential . . . communication channels.

The necessity of having a rationale or strategy of persuasion when encouraging innovation adoption is indicated by Milio

(1971, p. 164): "If you want to get [agencies] involved in something new, you have to show them what's in it for them." Summarizing the need for experimental manipulation of entry channels, reference group appeals, and other factors, Bettinghaus (1968, p. 23) comments:

> Factors central to persuasive communication from a receiver's point of view include variations within the source, within the message, difference in the channels used, and certain variations in the situation.

While the need for such marketing information has been noted widely, a review of the available literature supports a view that research findings in this area have been limited. Bettinghaus (1968), referring to his own previously stated hypotheses, observes that the evidence on this matter is "scanty." Similarly, Hage et al. (1971, p. 860) feel that "empirical studies which attempt to measure various aspects of communications in organizations are scarce." Our low-intensity study was developed in part as an attempt to rectify this lack of empirical evidence surrounding reference group appeals and entry channels, controlling other personal and organizational variables in the design. The first step was to specify or make operational both these concepts.

Reference Group Appeals

When we discuss reference group appeals we are entering an area of marketing theory referred to generally as "consumer behavior." Consumer behavior is concerned with the bases for consumer decision making and action regarding the obtaining of goods and services. According to Gist (1971), there are six basic determinants of consumer behavior: economic (purchasing power); demographic traits such as age, sex, and social class; reference group influences; learning process (consumer behavior as learned behavior); self-concept (how products relate to one's self-image); and the effects of influential personages. Reference group factors are generally considered one of the basic determinants and have a long-standing and prominent position in marketing research and practice. (A brief historical perspective on reference groups in marketing is found in Stafford, 1968.)

Much of the early work in developing reference group theory was conducted by social psychologists such as Herbert Hyman and Theodore Newcomb. A definition from the marketing literature offers a useful point of departure for our purposes:

> Reference groups are *those with which an individual identifies to the point where the group becomes a standard, a norm, or a point of reference for the individual.* In effect, the individual "refers" to such groups for standards of behavior and even for goals and personal values [Boone & Kurtz, 1977, p. 141; emphasis in original].

In this sense, reference groups may serve to legitimate, authenticate, or endorse certain products or innovations that are unfamiliar to a potential user. The reference group can be a potent stimulus to adoption or purchase. Reference groups may be large or small, formal or informal; and they may be groups in which an individual holds membership or to which he or she aspires. Thus they may have either psychological or empirical reality for an individual.

Standard television advertising approaches make heavy use of the reference group approach. Sports figures advocate certain beers to people who see themselves as sports fans. Teen movie idols extol certain brands of jeans for the younger set. Older, staid gentlemen point out the virtues of gentle laxatives to elderly viewers.

The message itself may be important in combination with the reference group connection. Roberto (1975), for example, used several different types of messages to encourage vasectomy, including: strengthening the man's marriage commitment; attaining a higher living standard; and relieving the wife of contraception burdens, leading to the full enjoyment of sex. He found that expectancy of full sexual enjoyment was the most influential message. In our study we standardized the message in order to focus on reference group features.

The structure and strategy of the message is also of consequence. Cohen (1964), drawing on a wide range of then existing research, hypothesized effects based upon whether the message is one-sided or two-sided, whether a conclusion is offered, and the order of presentation (either within a given communication or across successive communications). Again, our approach was standardized in order to isolate the one variable being studied. The message was one-sided, gave a conclusion, and placed the reference group appeal in a position of primacy in the order of presentation.

In a perceptive discussion of reference group influence, Engle et al. (1975) point out the dearth of published research upon which to base generalizations. They do, however, suggest some hypotheses and practical guidelines. They believe that low-status individuals, who feel less secure, may be more intensely affected by reference group pressures. Additionally, group influences may be especially potent in an informational vacuum, when the potential user has little information upon which to base action. Also, Engle et al. feel that product visibility may be the most important factor. The consumer is interested in knowing the specifics of a product in addition to opinions of the reference group. (In our study the reference group appeal message was accompanied by a product-handbook.) Finally, they emphasize the principle of different appeals to different users: "It can never be assumed that one appeal is appropriate for all" (Engle et al., 1975, p. 94).

The concern for reference group behavior in the marketing field is related to the marketing segmentation function; that is, identifying the characteristics of different submarkets in order to develop special channels and messages for linking with each. Yankelovich (1967) indicates that marketing approaches have typically relied too heavily upon easily available demographic data for developing promotional appeals. He suggests an alternative approach, designated "segmentation analysis." This approach employs primarily social psychological variables such as values, aesthetic concepts, attitudes, and individualized needs to describe and communicate with different markets. He goes on to provide practice documentation, demonstrating the effectiveness of such modes of promotional activity. The reference group notion is compatible with Yankelovich's advocacy of "nondemographic ways of segmenting markets." The question remaining is how to apply the reference group concept to a market composed of mental health professionals.

TYPES OF APPEAL

From a review of the sociological literature, we find that three basic role orientations have been identified in studies concerning professional human service workers: bureaucratic, professional, and community or client orientations. These may be summarized as follows:

> *Professional orientation* implies a high concern with professional values and standards, a *bureaucratic orientation* refers to a preoccupation with policies and norms of the employing agency, and *client orientation* connotes a primary attention to the needs of those served by the agency [Rothman, 1974, p. 83; emphasis in original].

These orientations may be expressed in terms of expectancies. Focal reference groups conveying expectations about job performance may be professional peers, agency superordinates, or client and community populations.

This type of threefold schema was employed by Epstein (1970a, 1970b, 1970c) in a series of studies examining the attitudes of social workers toward radicalism. Earlier, Wilensky (1967) used a similar format with a variation in terms: professional discipline, careerist, and client. In his work, Billingsley (1964) included the community dimension and found it could best be combined with the client concept. We have followed his formulation here.

For the purposes of this study, an appeal based on each role orientation was used to examine differential diffusion rates based on the appeal that was provided and the population group receiving the appeal. More specifically, each appeal was formulated as follows:

- *Bureaucratic Appeal:* Mental Health Agencies
  This appeal is to the practitioner's faith in *institutional* or *organizational legitimacy*. The practitioner is asked to move favorably

toward implementing policies and programs because the National Institute of Mental Health and the Family Service Association of America, and other established institutions of which he or she and his or her agency are a part, promote them.

- *Professional Appeal:* Mental Health Professions
  This appeal is to the practitioner's perceptions of his or her role *as a professional* in the mental health field. As a professional, the practitioner's responsibilities extend beyond community problems and institutional demands. The professional is concerned with current trends in research and with keeping abreast of new discoveries in the field. The appeal looks to professional and association colleagues as ultimate sources of authority in encouragement of innovative policies and programs.

- *Community/Client Appeal:* Community Groups and Key Citizens
  This appeal is to the practitioner's sense of *loyalty and responsiveness to local community groups and to clients* served by the agency. Meeting local needs and heeding the expressed articulation of need by those directly affected is the source of policy and program initiatives.

Copies of the brochures used in the study to convey the three different appeals appear in Appendix A.

PROFESSIONAL CRYSTALLIZATION AND APPEALS

The susceptibility of professionals to acceptance of an innovation can be increased by the application of an appeal consistent with the role orientation of the professional. Role orientation may be affected by the group's degree of professional crystallization:

> Crystallization of professional norms occurs when the occupation demands a full time effort, when the professional's knowledge is acquired in an institute attached to a university, and when the occupation is the basis for a professional association [Rothman, 1974, p. 162].

In mental health agencies four sets of professional groups predominate: psychiatrists, psychologists, social workers, and nurses. Of these, psychiatrists and psychologists are the most firmly established professional groups. As a result, they are presumed to have more concretely established professional norms than social workers and nurses, who have been designated sociologically as "semiprofessionals" (Etzioni, 1968). Accepting the validity of this assumption concerning professional norms leads to the conclusion that in agencies with a preponderance of established professionals, the professional appeal will have a strong impact for encouraging diffusion. The counterpart of this is that where "semiprofessionals" predominate, the bureaucratic appeal will most facilitate diffusion. The basis for this second statement rests with specific research findings that semiprofessionals are more disposed to accept *organizational* norms and constraints than are established professionals.

Illustratively, Billingsley (1964, pp. 403-404) states:

> Social workers in our sample are relatively more bureaucratic than professional in their moral evaluative orientations. The trend is in a direction opposite to that found in studies of other professional groups working in formal organizations. These other studies have tended to show that professional workers in these organizations were more oriented to the profession than to the agency itself.

Similarly, Epstein (1970c, p. 74) notes:

> Among social workers there seems to exist a hierarchy of normative commitments beginning with agency norms and ending with professional commitments.

Taebe (1972, p. 40) states:

> The agency is the source of the most compelling rewards—such as promotion and prestige—and thus largely shapes the social worker's orientation. Unfortunately, client groups are not likely to have much impact on his role definition.

It is thus reasonable, we believe, to hypothesize that "semiprofessional" social workers and nurses will be more responsive to the Bureaucratic Appeal than their more "professionally established" colleagues.

While we believed that the Professional Appeal would be most attractive to established professionals and the Bureaucratic Appeal to "semiprofessionals," we were on far more tenuous ground in our preassessments of the extent to which the Community/Client Appeal might work to encourage diffusion. Epstein (1970a, 1970b, 1970c) and Billingsley (1964) appeared to reach differing conclusions regarding the degree to which their social work subjects were client oriented. Epstein found his subjects to be moderately client oriented, while Billingsley determined that his subjects were rather low in this respect relative to the agency and professional orientations. Taebe (1972) supports the low rating given by Billingsley. Evidence provided by Hall (1968), however, suggests that social workers and nurses have a greater identity with a principle of service than do the more established professionals.

SYSTEM CHARACTERISTICS AND APPEAL

The mental health delivery system included in this study were community mental health centers and family service agencies, two of the main institutions providing counseling and therapy services to individuals and families in American communities. These human service organizations have different histories, structures, and operating arrangements (Rothman & Kay, 1977).

Family service agencies grow out of a social work tradition, having their origin in the "friendly visitor" philanthropic activities that originated in the last half of the nineteenth century (Ambrosino, 1977). Their focus is the family unit, their funding is generally from voluntary sources, and their personnel is composed largely of social work-trained persons; as a system they have a "semiprofessional" character.

Community mental health centers are a more recent human service form, having their major growth following World War II. They are more eclectic and diverse in the makeup of their professional cadre. They receive substantial funding from governmental sources. They consider the individual (and sometimes the community) as their primary beneficiary. Because of their composition of professionals from psychology, psychiatry, social work, and nursing, they can be presumed to have a mixed established professional/semiprofessional character.

It is possible to draw distinctions between the organizational climates that developed in each system. Based on our high-intensity fieldwork in both systems and a national data analysis of structural aspects of the two, distinguishing characteristics (in an ideal-type form) are summarized in Figure 3.1. Actually, the systems are less extreme and more mixed than this ideal-type format suggests. The distinctions are speculative and impressionistic rather than empirically constructed in a rigorous way. From this analysis we infer that the family service system is relatively more hierarchical and stable than the community mental health system and relatively more bureaucratic.

Based on the variable of *professional crystallization* and *organizational structure,* we developed the following main diffusion hypotheses:

- *For family service agencies, the bureaucratic appeal is likely to be strongest.*

    Rationale: The predominance of a "less established" professional staff and the existence of a somewhat hierarchical organizational structure. *The effects of the Community/Client Appeal are uncertain.*

- *For the community mental health centers, both bureaucratic and professional appeals are likely to be strong and rather equally matched.*

    Rationale: The typical employment of both "established" and "semiprofessional" service staff in this system should provide this mixed pattern of response. Because of the less hierarchical organizational structure, there may be a marginal advantage in favor of the Professional Appeal. *The effects of the Community/ Client Appeal will be weak.* Research evidence indicates conflicting responses to this appeal by the semiprofessional group and a weak response by established professionals. This should lead to an overall weak effect.

	Community Mental Health Centers	Family Service Agencies
General	turbulent fragmented changing experimental little continuity	staid uniform stable traditional much continuity

Leadership	weak control
	low level
	  of hierarchy
		strong control
		high level
		  of hierarchy

Structure	decentralized	Centralized

Composition
  of personnel
	heterogeneous
	  (diversified)
		homogeneous
		  (uniform)

Effects of
  outside
  environment
  (federal
  programs, etc.)
	strong effects
	responsive to
	  outside
		weak effects
		less responsive
		  to outside

Communication	poor or
	  disjointed
	  communications
		adequate and
		  regular
		  communications

Program	wide range of
	  types
	changing programs
		smaller range of
		  types
		stable programs

Clientele	wide range of
	  types
		smaller range of
		  types

Figure 3.1: Organizational Differences Between CMHCs and FSAAs, Based on Impressionistic Observations

We must point out that the field study did not involve designing separate diffusion campaigns using these hypotheses as marketing strategies. The state of knowledge, we thought, did not permit such a definitive approach. Rather, we used the different appeals with matched groups from the two systems and in a post hoc manner determined whether different subgroups within these two systems had responded differentially to the appeals. In the design of the study, we gathered background data on personal characteristics of agency personnel and structural features of organizational units. This afforded an opportunity to relate additional variables to the effects of different appeals.

APPEAL RELATED TO PERSONAL CHARACTERISTICS

There is a paucity of literature support for developing firm hypotheses concerning demographic characteristics of practitioners and professional role orientations. The development of hypotheses, therefore, for results obtained when associating appeal with specific practitioner characteristics should be viewed more as the development of "suppositions," extrapolations derived from logical deductions made by examining what bits of evidence are available in the literature. Some *subsidiary hypotheses* we developed were based on specific demographic or personal characteristics: *age, sex, education level, amount of professional experience,* and *professional identity.*

Age

For younger groups we surmised that the Community/Client Appeal might be most effective. Younger workers are most likely to be direct service workers (Epstein, 1970a, 1970b; Finch, 1976). This group struck us as potentially concerned with, and aware of, community/client interests. In a sense, they have not obtained the extensive professional training or had professional experience sufficient for them to acquire a strong professional orientation; nor have they worked in an agency setting long enough to acquire an acute bureaucratic orientation. *For older groups, however, we felt that both the Bureaucratic and Professional Appeals would predominate over the Community/Client Appeal.* This older group has had more opportunity to obtain a professional education and/or to internalize agency norms and standards during more extensive training and work experience (Weinbach, 1973).

Gender

Again, based on the limited literature base, estimates of differential diffusion rates based upon gender are tenuous. *For males we guessed that the Bureaucratic Appeal might be the most effective, while for females comparatively the Professional and Community/Client Appeals might be most likely to effect diffusion.* We reasoned that men in human service settings have traditionally tended to be highly career oriented and concerned with upward mobility. In fact, whether an artifact of our society or a reflection of strong career orientation, men have tended to rise to the higher administrative levels of social agencies. Hayes and Varley (1965) suggest that social work training, which is agency oriented in many respects, has a greater impact on the value orientation of male students than females. In contrast, women have been more likely to hold direct service positions, suggesting the likelihood of greater susceptibility to innovations that are encouraged by client-oriented appeals and to professional influences.

Education

It is generally felt that a professional role orientation will be adopted in direct proportion to the amount of professional training received (Rothman, 1974; Weinbach, 1973; Crocker & Brodie, 1974). Those practitioners, therefore, who have received the highest educational degrees should be more professionally oriented than those with lower education levels. We would expect, as a result, that those with lower education levels, lacking to a considerable extent a professional influence, would be more likely to look toward the agency for obtaining job norms, rewards, and satisfactions. This suggests that *those with higher levels of education should be more susceptible to the Professional Appeal, while those at lower levels of education should be more responsive to the Bureaucratic Appeal, and, because of the greater likelihood of their direct service involvement, to the Community/Client Appeal as well.*

Amount of Professional Experience

Increased professional experience may tend to reinforce professional norms. Increased experience may also bind one's loyalty to the employing agency. Professional experience, however, is cumulative, while employment with agencies varies and shifts during one's career. For this reason, we believed that the professional rather than the bureaucratic factor would be somewhat favored with increased work experience. In addition, increased professional experience brings status and resources to combat bureaucratic demands.

Rothman (1974, p. 167) provides a rationale: "Bureaucratic norms will predominate when professionals are vulnerable (small number, weak norms, [weak credentials], etc.) and when agency norms are strong." The hypothesis, accordingly, is: *For practitioners with greater professional experience Professional Appeals will be most effective; for professionals with less professional experience, Bureaucratic Appeals will be most effective. Additionally, those with less experience will be susceptible to Community/Client Appeals.* These are more likely to be direct service practitioners with many client and community contacts.

APPEAL RELATED TO STRUCTURAL FACTORS

As with personal traits, the hypotheses we developed for the use of appeals with specific agency background characteristics have a weak basis of support. Structural characteristics available for analysis included the size of the agency, presence of minority staff, use of nonprofessional practitioners, and extent of auxiliary professional staff.

Size of the Agency

The larger the organization, the more hierarchical it is likely to become, and the more bureaucratic will be the influences at work. However, larger agencies possess funds and resources with which to attract and employ larger numbers of professionals and professionals with higher levels of education and status (Pappenfort & Kilpatrick, 1967). This latter set of circumstances tends to enhance professional norms and influences. Larger organizational size thus gives accent to both bureaucratic and professional norms. Hence, *in larger agencies, the impact of Bureaucratic Appeals and Professional Appeals should be nearly equal. Professional Appeals may be marginally stronger because of the capability of professional norms to crystallize in such situations.* Because of the relative weakness of professional norms in smaller units, existing structural features will assure that *Bureaucratic Appeals will be most effective in small agencies.*

Presence of Minority Staff

In those agencies with a greater representation of minority staff members, we believed that the Community/Client Appeal would be more effective than in those agencies with a lower minority presence. The argument here is that the presence of minorities increases the likelihood that agency staff will be responsive to community interests (see Katan, 1974; Bartlett, 1974).

Nonprofessional Practitioners in the Agency

We were reasonably convinced that those practitioners who lacked professional training would be more responsive to either Bureaucratic or Community/Client Appeals compared to Professional Appeals. Such individuals are particularly vulnerable to agency ideology and demands. Thus *agencies with proportionally more nonprofessional practitioners will respond more strongly to Bureaucratic and Community/Client Appeals.*

Auxiliary Professional Staff in the Agency

Auxiliary staff in organizational maintenance roles, such as accountants, lawyers, and so forth, are unlikely to be oriented toward appeals provided by the mental health profession. Similarly, Community/Client Appeals would seem to have a reduced effect for this group as they would be unlikely to serve in direct service positions. As a result, we hypothesized that *an increased proportion of staff serving in such auxiliary positions would increase the tendency for Bureaucratic Appeals to be effective in these agencies.*

Point of Entry into the Organization

In this study three possible entry channels into agencies were delineated: *Executive, Training or Staff Development Specialist,* and *Special Interest Person.* Each had its own basis for selection:

- *Executive:* Considered to possess the most formal authority in an agency. However, it is possible that the Executive might have the greatest time restrictions in promoting new professional techniques. The Executive Entry was selected to measure the success of pursuing an Entry Channel at the top of the agency hierarchy.

- *Training Specialist:* While a staff development specialist might have only moderate authority or influence in an agency, this person could be potentially the most interested in obtaining and using new training materials. Training Entry was used as an indication of diffusion potential when entering in the middle of the agency hierarchy.

- *Special Interest Person:* The Special Interest Entry (for example, consultation and education director in community mental health agencies, director of family advocacy in family service agencies) was assumed to lack much formal authority but to have a strong interest in obtaining and using materials concerned with the establishment of specialized innovative techniques within that individual's functional sphere. The Special Interest Entry was considered to be a middle-level entry channel.

In considering the point-of-entry issue, marketing theory is of less immediate usefulness than it was for reference group appeals. In general, the issue has been most closely examined in a stream of studies investigating "organizational buying behavior." Several recent reviews of the field offer a helpful overview (Sheth, 1977; Nocosia & Wind, 1977; Bonoma et al., 1977; Thomas & Wind, 1977).

Organizational buying behavior is hardly a trivial matter, as Kotler (1982, p. 252) points out:

> Nonprofit organizations not only market to individuals but also to organizations. Here are some examples:
>
> * A performing arts group needs a foundation grant to support a new experimental theater. It must know how to identify likely foundations and their "buying criteria" for choosing among the various proposals they receive.
>
> * A large hospital is trying to convince nearby hospitals to share services—such as laundry and lab work—to bring down costs. The hospital is also trying to convince the local health systems agency to approve its application to open a new burn unit to serve the area.
>
> * A national association needs a strategy to convince its local chapters to increase membership dues so that more money would be available to lobby for legislative reforms.
>
> * Mississippi's Industrial Development Department needs a plan to attract companies to locate new plants in Mississippi. Meanwhile, Mississippi's Department of Tourism is trying to convince major hotel chains to locate new hotels in Mississippi's major cities.
>
> Thus, nonprofit organizations get involved in selling goods, services and ideas to other organizations. They need to understand the buying organizations' needs, resources, policies, and buying procedures. They need to take into account . . . considerations not normally found in consumer marketing.

Organizational buying behavior, as the term indicates, is concerned with the purchase of new materials and services by units and systems, particularly among industrial firms. In reviewing the body of knowledge thus far accumulated, Wind (1978, p. 164) comments on its limitations:

> One can draw very few substantive generalizations as to which variables would have what effect under what conditions. . . . [There

has been] lack of systematic effort . . . to build a cumulative body of substantive findings about organizational buying behavior and its determinants.

Nevertheless, certain perspectives are of use. Related to point of entry, there have been a considerable number of studies dealing with buying centers—that is, loci within the organization where purchasing decisions are made. Rather than dealing with the level within the organization where such centers are situated, adoption or acquisition has been associated with variables such as cosmopolitan orientation, risk-taking propensity, younger age, entrepreneurial orientation, and self-confidence. One might extrapolate concerning the level of the organization where such attributes are likely to be concentrated. These studies, however, tend to confirm point of entry as a useful variable to investigate.

In industry, buying centers have been found to be largely multiperson aggregates (Choffray & Lilien, 1976; Grashof & Wind, 1975). This may possibly be a variation from the condition in the human services. Purchasing innovations in industry may require much larger expenditures of financial resources and thus call upon collective judgments to a greater degree. Whether collective or individual decisions are implicated may vary with the specific innovation, depending on the scope of resource investment required and the degree to which the innovation requires an organizational response or individual responses on the part of single potential users (see Chapter 10 for a further discussion of this issue). It was our assumption in this study that an individual decision at the point-of-entry position would be sufficient to foster diffusion. The school of marketing research suggests that this is an area meriting further investigation. Other typical areas of investigation in that school that could profitably be transposed to human service organizations include the following: interorganizational linkages between the diffusing agency and the adopting agency; bargaining and negotiating procedures; how decisions are made within the adopting agency (including conflict resolution in the organization); effects of perceived risk; and delineating a range of criteria used in purchasing decisions.

Organizational buying behavior studies in marketing seem to be more helpful in suggesting other variables to consider rather than in offering hypotheses that clarify or refine the variables we have chosen to investigate. These studies may indicate interacting or intervening variables relative to point-of-entry considerations. One can anticipate that knowledge from the marketing field may be of more utility for our purposes in the near future. Wind (1978, p. 182) states:

> The scope of organizational behavior studies should be broadened beyond the traditional focus on industrial firms to include other organizations (e.g., hospitals, schools, government institutions) and, in particular, other types of organizations as small (not only large) [and] nonprofit (not for profit).

Wind also suggests expanding the concept of products to be acquired to include services and R&D knowledge and technology.

THE EXECUTIVE AS DIFFUSION COMMUNICATOR

In the sociological organizational diffusion literature numerous studies are available with regard to the chief administrator position as a stimulus for innovation. Unfortunately, findings are conflicting (Hage & Aiken, 1967, 1969; Palumbo, 1969; Mohr, 1969; Alvarez, 1968). The chief organizational officer is in a key position (potentially) to legitimate and enforce new procedures and practices. The individual holding this position often has the authority to act. Because of concern for maintenance needs of the organization, however, and a multiplicity of cross-pressures, one's concern is often with stability rather than change. The particular attitude of an administrator toward innovation in general, or toward a given innovation, will likely affect the extent to which this individual is a facilitating factor in instituting new practices. Mohr (1969) found that the attitude of the chief executive was crucial in the introduction of "progressive programming" in public health departments. In addition, as Tannenbaum and Bachman (1966) indicate, the chief executive is in a more favorable position than others to break away from established organizational norms.

MIDDLE-LEVEL PERSONNEL AS DIFFUSION COMMUNICATORS

Some scholars view the operational-level opinion leader as the most critical point in the flow of communication and as an agent of diffusion of innovation (Katz & Lazarsfeld, 1955; Glaser, 1971; Hage & Dewar, 1971; Havelock & Havelock, 1973; Hage et al., 1971; Marcus & House, 1973; Westley, 1971). They assume that the flow of communication will most likely be horizontal, and the chances of innovation adoption are higher here because of close contact with colleagues. This literature seems to be suggesting, then, that the most effective entry point would be at the middle of the organization through a person who is removed from direct authority influence, but whose control of lateral networks of communication may influence a large number of people. This presumes, of course, that sufficient aggregate individual change will produce system change, a debatable but useful presumption for the purposes of our marketing effort. It also assumes possession of a sufficient degree of authority or the existence of a flat organizational structure that permits influence to be exerted laterally in the organization.

The literature argues equally forcefully for a top or a middle channel of entry. With this in mind, a theoretical formulation by Litwak et al. (1970) and study findings by Fairweather and his associates (1974) suggest a direction for an alternative hypothesis. Litwak et al. hold that in agencies having a collegial or "human relations" structure, as is typical of most mental health agencies, influence is rather diffuse and innovations may enter effectively at any point in the organization, top or middle. While community mental health centers and family service agencies do not have identical structures, they are both in the middle range of hierarchy and of human relations character, especially when compared to the military, police departments, large corporations, or even a social welfare bureaucracy such as the Social Security Administration. Within this middle-range area, family service agencies are in the bureaucratic direction to a greater degree than are mental health centers. In their research, Fairweather et al. (1974) discovered that alternative entry channels gave equal results in diffusing an innovative program to mental health hospitals, consistent with the Litwak et al. theory.

This leads to the following major hypothesis:

> *Points of entry at different levels of the organization involving the positions of Executive, Training and Staff Development Specialist, and Special Interest Person will yield equivalent diffusion results. This will be consistent for both the community mental health and family service systems (although the Executive Entry may be marginally stronger for the latter because of its somewhat more bureaucratic structure).*

Combined Appeal/Entry Strategy

One other question of interest was the possibility that effects of the two independent variables, Appeal and Entry, might interact on one another. If such interactions do occur and are significant, then we guess that the mechanisms might be something like the following:

- *Executive:* Presumably, his or her major concern is the agency. In that case *the Bureaucratic Appeal ought to be most effective.*

- *Training and Staff Development Specialist:* We assume he or she is especially interested in professionally supported training techniques. In that case *the Professional Appeal ought to prove the most effective.*

- *Special Interest Person:* As his or her primary function or interest in this study is community education and advocacy, *the Community/ Client Appeal ought to yield the greatest diffusion.*

| | | Reference Group Appeal | |
	Bureaucratic	Professional	Community/ Client
Executive	X		
Entry Training Specialist		X	
Special Interest			X

Figure 3.2: Hypothetical Optimal Appeals for Different Points of Entry

Crossruffing appeal and entry, this hypothesis allows a visually tidy depiction, which is presented in Figure 3.2. For this speculation there was the least amount of research evidence. It was subjected to empirical testing in a nationwide, action-research, experimental field study together with the full set of speculative hypotheses. The design of that investigation will be the focus of the next chapter.

References

Alvarez, R. Informal reaction to deviance in simulated work organization: A laboratory experiment. *American Sociological Review,* 1968, 33(6).

Ambrosino, S. Family services: Family service agencies. In National Association of Social Workers, *Encyclopedia of Social Work* (Vol. 1). Washington, DC: National Association of Social Workers, 1977.

Bartlett, R. S. Ethnicity, professionalism and black paternalism: Implications for social welfare services. *Journal of Sociology and Social Welfare,* 1974, 1(3), 101-111.

Bettinghaus, E. P. *Persuasive communication.* New York: Holt, Rinehart & Winston, 1968.

Billingsley, A. Bureaucratic and professional orientation patterns in social casework. *Social Service Review,* 1964, 38(4), 33-40.

Bonoma, T. V., Zaltman, G., & Johnston, W. J. *Industrial buying behavior.* Cambridge, MA: Marketing Science Institute, 1977.

Boone, L., & Kurtz, D. L. *Foundations of marketing.* Hinsdale, IL: Dryden, 1977.

Choffray, J. M. & Lilien, G. L. *Models of the multiperson choice process with application to the adoption of industrial products.* Sloan School, MIT, working paper 861-876, June 1976.

Cohen, A. R. *Attitude change and social influence.* New York: Basic Books, 1964.

Crocker, L. M., & Brodie, B. J. Development of a scale to assess student nurses' views of the professional nursing role. *Journal of Applied Psychology,* 1974, 59(3), 233-235.

Engle, J. F., Wales, H. G., Warshaw, M. R. *Promotional strategy* (3rd ed). Homewood, IL: Irwin, 1975.

Epstein, I. Careers, professionalization and radicalism. *Social Service Review,* June 1970, pp. 123-131. (a)

Epstein, I. Professional role orientation and conflict strategies. *Social Work,* October 1980, pp. 87-92. (b)

Epstein, I. Professionalization, professionalism and social-worker radicalism. *Journal of Health and Social Behavior,* March 1970, pp. 67-77. (c)

Etzioni, A. *The semi-professionals and their organizations: Teachers, nurses, social workers.* New York: Macmillan, 1969.

Fairweather, G. W., Sanders, D. H., & Tornatzky, L. G. *Creating change in mental health organizations.* New York: Pergamon, 1974.

Finch, W. A. Social workers vs. bureaucracy. *Social Work,* September 1976, pp. 370-380.

Glaser, E. M., & Ross, H. L. *Increasing the utilization of applied research results* (final report to the National Institute of Mental Health). Los Angeles: Human Interaction Institute, 1971.

Gist, R. R. *Marketing and society: A conceptual introduction.* New York: Holt, Rinehart & Winston, 1971.

Grashof, J., & Wind, Y. *The buying center: An empirical evaluation of roles and responsibilities in the purchase of scientific and technical information services.* Wharton School, University of Pennsylvania, working paper, November 1975.

Hage, J., & Aiken, M. Program change and organizational properties. *American Journal of Sociology,* 1967, 72(5), 503-519.

Hage, J., & Aiken, M. Routine technology, social structure and organizational goals. *Administrative Science Quarterly,* 1969, 14(3).

Hage, J., Aiken, M., & Marrett, C. B. Organizational structure and communications. *American Sociological Review,* October 1971, pp. 860-871.

Hage, J., & Dewar, R. *The prediction of organizational performance: The case of program innovation.* Paper presented at the American Sociological Association annual meetings, Denver, Colorado, August 1971.

Hall, R. H. Professionalization and bureaucratization. *American Sociological Review,* 1968, 33(1), 92-104.

Havelock, D. G., & Havelock, M. C. *Training for change agents.* Ann Arbor: Center for Research Utilization of Scientific Knowledge, Institute for Social Research, University of Michigan, 1973.

Hayes, D. D., & Varley, B. K. Impact of social work education on students' values. *Social Work,* 1965, 10(3), 40-46.

Katan, J. The utilization of indigenous workers in human service organizations. In Y. Hasenfeld & R. English (Eds.), *Human service organizations.* Ann Arbor: University of Michigan Press, 1974.

Katz, E., & Lazarsfeld, P. *Personal influence: The part played by people in the flow of mass communication.* New York: Macmillan, 1955.

Kotler, P. *Marketing for nonprofit organizations* (2nd ed.). Englewood Cliffs, NJ: Prentice-Hall, 1982.

Litwak, E., Figueira-McDonough, J., Agemian, J., Hamilton, G., & Rhoades, G. *Towards the multi-factor theory and practice of linkages between formal organizations.* Washington, DC: Social and Rehabilitation Services Department, U.S. Department of Health, Education and Welfare, 1970.

Marcus, P. M., & House, J. S. Exchange between superiors and subordinates in large organizations. *Administrative Science Quarterly,* 1973, 18, 209-222.

Milio, N. Health care organizations and innovation. *Journal of Health and Social Behavior,* June 1971, pp. 163-173.

Mohr, L. B. Determinants of innovation in organizations. *American Political Science Review,* March 1969, pp. 111-126.

Nicosia, F., and Wind, Y. Behavioral models of organizational buying processes. In F. Nicosia and Y. Wind (Eds.), *Behavioral models for market analysis: Foundations of marketing action.* Hinsdale, IL: Dryden, 1977.

Palumbo, D. J. Power and role specificity in organizational theory. *Public Administration Review,* 1969, 29(3) 237-248.

Pappenfort, D. M., & Kilpatrick, D. M. Opportunities for physically handicapped children: A study of attitudes and practices in settlements and community centers. *Social Science Review,* 1967, 41(2), 179-188.

Roberto, E. L. *Strategic decision-making in a social program.* Lexington, MA: D.C. Heath, 1975.

Rothman, J. *Planning and organizing for social change: Action principles from social science research.* New York: Columbia University Press, 1974.

Rothman, J., & Kay, T. Community mental health centers and family service agencies. *Social Work Research and Abstracts,* 1977, 13(4), 10-16.

Sheth, N. Recent developments in organizational buying behavior. In A. G. Woodside, J. N. Sheth, & M. Bennett (Eds.), *Consumer and industrial buying behavior.* New York: Elsevier North-Holland, 1977.

Stafford, J. E. Preference theory as a conceptual framework for consumer decisions. In R. L. King (Eds.), *Marketing and the new science of planning* (1968 Fall Conference Proceedings). Chicago: American Marketing Association, 1968.

Taebe, D. A. Strategies to make bureaucrats responsive. *Social Work,* November 1972, pp. 38-43.

Tannenbaum, A. S., & Bachman, J. G. Attitude uniformity and role in a voluntary organization. *Human Relations,* 1966, 19(3), 309-323.

Thomas, R., & Wind, Y. *On the status of organizational buying behavior.* Wharton School, University of Pennsylvania, working paper, 1977.

Ward, C. D., Seboda, B. C., Morris, V. B. Influence through personal and nonpersonal channels of communication. *Journal of Psychology,* September 1974, pp. 135-140.

Weinbach, R. W. Identification with the social work and mental health professions as factors relating to social worker job satisfaction and job performance: an inquiry into the value of the interprofessional model (Doctoral dissertation, University of Michigan—Ann Arbor). *Dissertation Abstracts International,* 1973. (University Microfilms No. 73-2156).

Westley, B. H. Communication and social change. *American Behavioral Scientist,* May-June 1971, pp. 719-743.

Wilensky, H. *Organizational intelligence.* New York: Basic Books, 1967.

Wind, Y. Organizational buying behavior. In G. Zaltman & T. V. Bonoma (Eds.), *Review of marketing 1978.* Pittsburgh: American Marketing Association, Marketing Science Institute, and Graduate School of Business, 1978.

Yankelovich, D. New criteria for market segmentation. In P. R. Cateroa & L. Richardson (Eds.), *Readings in marketing: The qualitative and quantitative areas.* New York: Meredith, 1967.

CHAPTER 4

STUDYING MASS COMMUNICATIONS SOCIAL MARKETING

A Brief Look Forward

In this chapter we describe the methodology of the low-intensity study. We begin by arguing for the usefulness of natural field experiments over laboratory methods in a study of this kind. We describe our sample selection and the assignment of 595 organizations within a 9-cell grid that interrelates the 3 appeals and the 3 points of entry. We address the question of attaching a charge for the innovative product (the handbook) as an aspect of general design.

We review the rather complex mailing procedure, including titles used to reach the appropriate point-of-entry positions at which we aimed. Two types of substudies are described: the dissemination substudy, which deals with the *ordering of handbooks* (that is, their distribution) and the utilization substudy, which deals with the *actual use of the handbooks* in the field. We describe how we employed a "Depth of Utilization" (DU) scale as a measure of the extent of use of the handbook. We also present the different measures employed for gauging dissemination and utilization rates. We conclude with a description of data analysis problems and procedures.

General Design Features

The research design used for the low-intensity marketing effort was consistent with those controlled field studies proposed by marketing and mass communication researchers (Venkatesen & Holloway, 1970; Bass et al., 1968; Cox, 1966; Achenbaum, 1974). Haskins (1968, p. 7), for example, states that "proper experimental design in naturalistic conditions is necessary to study the effects of communications." We drew in part on communications and marketing research because what we were dealing with included important communications aspects. This particular body of research appeared to offer fertile ground for guiding our efforts. An experimental approach is, of course, necessary to ensure systematic observation and testing with regard to the investigation. We hoped we would be able to attribute any effects of dissemination or utilization to the specific treatment variables we selected, namely, reference group appeal, point of entry into the organization, or a combination of both appeal and entry. The use of a naturalistic environment for our research, we felt, would facilitate the generalizability of our research to the "real world," even though we recognized the preliminary nature of this research. We also wished to give a trial to established marketing tools and procedures to see how they apply in a social marketing context.

We have expressed our preference for the field study. In marketing research the two main streams of research effort have consisted of laboratory experiments and controlled field experiments. Cox and Enis (1969) present an incisive analysis of the advantages and disadvantages of each of these approaches in the advertising field. The laboratory setting is artificial and abstract, but the situation provides rather unambiguous data about a limited number of discrete variables. Experiments conducted in the field deal with realistic phenomena, but data tend to be ambiguous because of the complexity and fluidity of the environment in which they are gathered. It might be said that laboratory experiments generally have higher internal validity and field experiments higher external validity. Results in the latter case can more readily be transferred to other situations. From a more practical standpoint, field experiments are more elaborate and more difficult to implement, and require more time and resources to obtain results. Ray (1978) suggests that field experimentation is in a sense a higher order of research in that it may be viewed as following more preliminary, variable-defining studies conducted in the laboratory. He goes on to point out that the behavioral and social sciences have lagged behind in carrying out this kind of dynamic research:

> Few behavioral field experiments have been done compared to the number which have been and are being carried out in advertising. Field experimentation has long been a tool of advertising research [Ray, 1978, p. 122].

There has been a lack of intervention-type action-research in the school of diffusion studies. By contrast the American Marketing Association has reported that 81 percent of the leading manufacturing firms had established formal marketing research departments (Twerdt, 1973).

In this social marketing study we chose to follow the pattern of the marketing field, examining intervention outcomes in the "real-world" context, while maximizing controls to the extent this was feasible. Those who participated in our study received all material related to our social product, the practitioner's handbook, in the normal course and setting of their specific job situations. Defined controls and careful record keeping, however, permitted a high level of monitoring of distribution and use in this substudy.

Later in this chapter, we will discuss the various treatment conditions in considerable detail. As a general overview, however, we employed three different appeals and three different entry points, as shown in Figure 4.1.

The use of this treatment design had the advantage of permitting an analysis of appeal and entry either separately or in a combined format. This basic treatment grid was employed for analyzing the dissemination modes and assessing the extent to which the social product was used by human service practitioners from those agencies in which the handbooks were disseminated.

The analysis plan permitted the study of possible effects of appeal and entry on both dissemination and utilization of the practitioner's handbook. A point of interest concerned whether

		Bureaucratic	Appeal Professional	Community/Client
Entry	Executive	1	4	7
	Training Specialist	2	5	8
	Special Interest	3	6	9

Figure 4.1:   Treatment Design

dissemination and utilization behavior would coincide or vary. We had no reason to assume that the hypotheses we developed would differ for dissemination and utilization, but the design allowed us to examine that question. Furthermore, the plan allowed us to identify possibly important agency and practitioner characteristics in which appeal and entry may produce important effects. The remainder of this chapter will describe the study design and analysis plan. Findings will be presented in Chapter 5.

Field Procedures

SAMPLE SELECTION

To reiterate, the two agency systems included in this study were community mental health centers (CMHCs) supported by the National Institute of Mental Health and family service agencies that maintained affiliation with the Family Service Association of America (FSAAs). We selected these two systems for both theoretical and practical reasons. First, within the field of mental health these are the two largest delivery systems that have a community-based orientation. We felt, based on our earlier work, that the practitioner's handbook was particularly appropriate for community-oriented programs. As a matter of practical interest to us, we had access to numerous agency background characteristics that were available from both systems' national offices. As we have already discussed in our review of the diffusion literature, many researchers have identified specific agency structural characteristics related to size and so forth that affect the diffusion process. Second, we felt that by having two separate systems included in our research effort, we would be able to assess the extent to which our findings might tend to be generalizable—that is, to determine if, perhaps, there were unique patterns of dissemination and utilization distinct to given systems or if there might be more overarching diffusion configurations embracing more than one system.

TREATMENT ASSIGNMENT

Our procedure for agency selection was fairly straightforward. First, the universe of CMHCs and FSAAs was considered. This universe of agencies was obtained from the 1975 *Directory of Federally Funded Community Mental Health Centers,* published by the National Institute of Mental Health, and the 1975 *FSAA Directory of Member Agencies,* issued by the publications department of the Family Service Association. CMHC and FSAA agencies were excluded in the eight U.S. cities that were involved in our high-intensity study (Chapters 6-9). All other agencies within the same city as a high-intensity agency were likewise excluded. We could not overlook the possibility that previous contact with the handbook, even indirect contact, might have increased initial practitioner interest or given rise to negative predispositions. As we wanted to ensure that all agencies had their initial contact with the handbook according to our predetermined study procedure, we excluded such potentially contaminated agencies. Additional deletions were made among those new "start-up" CMHC agencies that did not have an established staff and program and among FSAAs that had dropped FSAA membership or were actually only a part of a larger, central agency or were located in Canada. The total number of agencies selected for the study was 595: 335 CMHCs

TABLE 4.1   Distribution of CMHCs by Cells

CMHCs	Cell									Total
	1	2	3	4	5	6	7	8	9	
Size of Staff										
0-6	0	0	1	1	0	0	0	0	0	2
7-12	2	1	1	1	1	1	1	2	1	11
13-25	5	6	6	5	6	5	5	6	6	50
26-49	13	10	11	12	12	13	13	12	11	107
50+	18	18	19	19	19	19	19	17	17	165
Total	38	35	38	38	38	38	38	37	35	335

and 260 FSAAs. Discussions with national and regional representatives of both systems assisted us in developing and applying these criteria.

Each agency selected was assigned to a specific treatment cell (Figure 4.1) by stratified random assignment. We placed a limit of 12 on the number of handbooks that could be sent to each agency. Given that the handbooks were free and that our resources were not unlimited, we wanted to assure that each agency, regardless of size, would have the opportunity to order an equal number of handbooks.

We assigned agencies to each cell by size. This was to guarantee an equivalent aggregate size distribution in each cell. We also ensured that each treatment cell had approximately equal numbers both of CMHCs and of FSAAs. Tables 4.1 and 4.2 give the distribution among the cells.

It is obvious that the distribution of staff size is skewed. This is a function of the way the two kinds of agencies are structured, and not a sampling selection artifact. CMHCs are simply much larger, on the whole, than FSAAs.

We considered and rejected the idea of charging a modest fee for the handbooks. Discussions with agency representatives convinced us that even a small charge of fifty cents or a quarter per handbook might require budgeting procedures equivalent to

TABLE 4.2   Distribution of FSAAs by Cells

FSAAs	Cell									Total
	1	2	3	4	5	6	7	8	9	
Size of Staff										
0-6	8	8	8	6	7	8	6	8	8	67
7-12	9	6	7	9	9	7	9	9	8	73
13-25	9	9	9	7	7	9	9	8	9	76
26-49	2	4	4	3	4	2	4	4	4	31
50+	2	1	1	2	1	2	2	1	1	13
Total	30	28	29	27	28	28	30	30	30	260

those used for large purchases. As we wished to optimize the response rate for analysis purposes (that is, to obtain sufficient numbers of responses in each cell), we distributed the handbooks at no cost.

The area of pricing is of crucial importance in marketing theory. McCarthy (1968) postulates price as one of the four basic components of marketing. Marketers have taken a number of different approaches to pricing, including cost-oriented pricing, profit-based pricing, competition-oriented pricing, and demand-oriented pricing (Enis, 1974). DeLozier (1976) indicates that pricing should be related to factors such as the characteristics of the product, of the consumers, and of the objectives of the specific marketing situation. This broad approach is useful in viewing the factor of price in social marketing.

Typically, in social marketing, profit is not a key consideration in carrying out a diffusion program. The objective is to disseminate an idea, program, or technique essential to the benefit of a wide variety of potential users, that is, to promote the general welfare. Thus frequently no fee is attached to the product, or the fee is set at a level sufficient merely to recover the cost of producing and disseminating the product.

Nevertheless, a sensitive social marketing program should recognize noneconomic costs to the potential user of adopting innovative practices or products. Some of these have been spelled out by Kotler and Zaltman (1971). They define price as the "costs that the buyer must accept in order to obtain the product" (p. 9). In addition to monetary costs, these include opportunity costs, energy costs, and psychic costs. For example, in using a new intervention technique, the human service professional must take into account the opportunities for service that would be lost should the innovation not be effective, the energy involved in learning a new way of work, and the psychic discomfort associated with giving up a familiar and dependable method for one that is, perhaps, strange and unpredictable. The potential user, accordingly, weighs a variety of factors in the process of making an adoption decision. Kotler and Zaltman (1971, p. 9) state:

> The marketing man's approach to pricing the social product is based on the assumption that members of a target audience perform a cost-benefit analysis when considering the investment of money, time or energy in the issue. They somehow process the major costs, and the strength of their motivation to act is directly related to the magnitude of the excess benefit.

Our consideration of attaching a charge to the handbook was based on such a perspective.

MAILING PROCEDURE

We established a carefully controlled mailing procedure to assure that the agencies received the appropriate treatments as determined by the sampling plan. Each of the 595 agencies was sent a packet of materials that included a professionally designed, four-page, two-color brochure describing the handbook and containing that agency's assigned appeal (Bureaucratic, Professional, or Community/Client). Also included in the packet were one copy of the handbook, a letter of description and introduction, an order form permitting the ordering of up to 12 additional copies of the handbook, and a postage-paid return envelope.

Each packet was directed to one of the preselected entrý channels: Executive, Training Specialist, or Special Interest Person. This was done by addressing the material to the entry person's title, as the actual names of recipients were generally unknown to us. To reinforce the point-of-entry position, we indicated a general title and gave additional emphasis by writing "ATTENTION," followed by a description of the position or role. We selected titles after consulting with NIMH and FSAA national and regional staff. This ensured that the titles we used were consistent with agency terminology. Figure 4.2 presents the general titles and descriptions selected.

The order forms requesting additional copies required an additional dissemination procedure. The form specifically requested the names of those who would receive the handbooks. For each of these, we assembled a packet that contained a brochure with an appeal identical to that sent to the initial agency entry person, a handbook, and a letter explaining the reason for the mailing. All of the assembled packets for a particular agency were then sent to the agency person who submitted the order. In a cover letter we asked that individual to distribute the packets to the relevant staff. Irregular order forms (forms from agencies requesting handbooks but failing to supply the names of the recipients, agencies ordering more than 12 handbooks, and so on) were returned to the agency with a note explaining why we were unable to fill the order. We encouraged the agency to resubmit a corrected form. We used an arbitrary cutoff date for filling handbook requests of approximately three months from the date of the original agency mailing.

In all, 2688 names were submitted to us on order forms. These we considered our total sample for analyzing both the extent of use of our product (the handbook) and the extent to which entry or/and appeal might be associated with that use. We achieved a 38.1 percent return on questionnaires (N = 1025), which defined our data base for analysis.

	To Executive	To Training Specialist	To Community Specialist
CMHCs	Executive Director	Coordinator of Staff Training and Development	Director of Consultation and Education
FSAAs	Executive director Services	Director of Professional Services	Family Advocate–Community Services Coordinator
Position/ Role Descrip- tion	Both	Attention: Chief Administrative Officer	Attention: In-Service Training Specialist	Attention: Community Outreach Specialist

Figure 4.2: Entry Titles and Descriptions

The guidelines presented in the handbook encouraged applications in short-term situations. Our previous experience persuaded us that three months was a sufficient length of time for practitioners to work with the guidelines and to provide us with sufficient, measurable results of application. We used a specially constructed questionnaire to measure the degree of utilization (see Appendix B). This questionnaire, individually addressed and mailed to each practitioner receiving a handbook, included personal background items, a letter reminding him or her that this follow-up had been mentioned in previous communications, and a postage-paid return envelope. About two weeks after this mailing, we sent a reminder postcard to those who had not yet returned their questionnaires.

We worked closely with a commercial advertising agency in developing the brochure. The tear-off return postcard, layout, pictures, distinctive project logo on all materials, and so forth, were produced through this firm. We drew on all the resources and expertise of the advertising agency. We retained creative control, however, over style, format, and content to assure that these would be consistent with the purposes of the study and the presumed values and outlook of human service professionals. Though we held veto power on all matters, we were not obliged to exercise it, as adequate communication and collaboration developed between research and advertising personnel.

The Dissemination Substudy

DATA ACQUISITION

As stated, each of the 595 agencies was assigned to 1 of 9 possible treatment cells: 3 possible appeals by 3 possible entry channels. Included in our data collection procedure was the matching of all project-acquired, agency data with background characteristics (such as staff size, agency expenditures, and so on). These data were made available from yearly agency questionnaires compiled by the national offices of NIMH and FSAA. We did not have data on personal characteristics of entry individuals.

MEASURING DISSEMINATION:
THE HANDBOOK DISSEMINATION RATIO

With our data in hand, we turned our attention to developing a means for comparing dissemination levels from each appeal, entry, and agency characteristic of interest. This proved somewhat more difficult than we had originally anticipated.

Ray (1978, p. 123) is one of many investigators who express a serious concern over possible bias that can be created by measurement effects:

> The advantage of the field experiment is that the advertising is exposed in a natural way in a natural setting with all the crucial field variables operating. It is important not to let the measurement requirement spoil the naturalness.

One technique suggested for overcoming this problem is to develop unobtrusive measures whenever and wherever possible. Ideally, there should be no perceptible relationship between communications made with the study sample and the measurement of their subsequent behavior. In the development of a measure for comparing dissemination levels for treatment groups, therefore, we were interested in measuring dissemination while minimizing possible observation bias. As the central issue of the dissemination process was to increase the distribution of the practitioner handbooks, we were interested in the extent to which each treatment technique resulted in subsequent handbooks ordered. No information outside of that request on the original handbook order form was necessary, as the number of handbooks ordered by an agency was ascertained simply by counting the number of names listed on the order form itself.

The specific measure we developed to indicate effectiveness of obtaining handbook orders we called the "Handbook Dissemination Ratio" (HDR): the ratio of the aggregate number of handbooks ordered by a subsample of agencies exposed to a given diffusion approach relative to the total number of handbooks that could possibly be ordered by these agencies (the number of agencies in the subsample times 12, the maximum order permitted per agency). The formula we used for this score was:

$$\frac{\text{aggregate number of handbooks ordered in cell}}{\text{total number of agencies in cell} \times 12} = \text{HDR}$$

The measure of initial interest in receiving material has a commonsense interpretation, that is, out of all handbooks that could have been ordered within a treatment cell, what percentage was actually ordered?

DATA ANALYSIS STRATEGY

Having devised the data collection and measurement schemes for our investigation of the dissemination process, we attacked the task of selecting an appropriate data analysis strategy. We will discuss our analysis procedures in some detail as we present the results of our studies. For now, however, we offer this general overview.

We determined to use the HDR measure as a descriptive indicator of trends. At the same time, we elected to use a contingency table analysis for hypothesis testing and for obtaining significance levels. For the contingency table analysis the number of handbook orders received from each agency was the dependent variable. Our independent variables were Appeal and Entry. We also examined the combination of Appeal and Entry.

As contingency tables require mutually exclusive categories, our dependent variable was divided into three levels: (1) No Order Received, (2) Less than the Maximum Possible Ordered (from 1 to 11), and (3) the Maximum Possible (12) Ordered. Although agencies were further analyzed by stratifying agency background characteristics, the basic contingency table analysis format is shown in Figure 4.3, using Appeal as an example of an independent variable.

While the contingency or frequency table analysis is not a direct test for differences in HDRs among treatment groups, a relationship does exist between the two. As indicated in a contingency table, those treatment cells that obtain higher

Appeal	0 Books	1-11 Books	12+ Books
Bureaucratic			
Professional			
Community/Client			

Figure 4.3:   Contingency Table Analysis Format

levels of handbook orders than expected would additionally receive the highest HDR. The calculation of the expected number of orders for a treatment cell was based on the assumption that there was no relationship between the factors investigated, given the existing (total) orders received. The contingency table and its associated statistics (maximum likelihood and chi square) were selected for hypothesis testing because of the categorical nature of much of the data that precluded the use of alternative analysis techniques requiring more rigid underlying assumptions regarding the nature of the data.

In summary, then, it was our intention to integrate the results of both the contingency tables and the Handbook Dissemination Ratios. While significant relationships are indicated by the contingency tables, the HDR assists in showing more clearly the direction of significant results. In general, the ratios we will present in our discussion were shown to be significant by the contingency tables. We will also offer some selected nonsignificant ratios to facilitate our discussion of overall trends.

The Utilization Substudy

The second major aspect of our low-intensity, mass marketing study was to focus on the extent to which practitioners actually *used* the social product we supplied. Obviously, there are a number of levels or degrees of use that can occur. It is equally obvious that the adoption of innovations is not a simple matter. Kuehnel and Eckman (1976), for example, view adoption as a complex process of social learning (see also Rice & Rogers, 1980). On the one hand, practitioners who received our handbook might have only skimmed the material. On the other, they might have completed the suggested guideline implementations with high levels of success. Or, their involvement with the material might have ended at any point in between. It was our intent to make some assessment of the degree of utilization that took place once the handbooks were distributed and to concentrate on any possible effects that the three main independent variables may have had on this level of utilization.

QUESTIONNAIRE DEVELOPMENT

The development of an evaluation instrument was essential for assessing the relative effect of each diffusion technique we employed in our low-intensity study. Our central concern was the "depth of utilization" of the new practice techniques explained in the handbook. This can be thought of as a continuum of utilization, and it was our intention to rank the importance of these various levels of guideline implementation relative to complete implementation. A variety of data assisted us in this effort. Besides the data concerned with guideline implementations and diffusion approaches, we also collected a variety of practitioner demographic data.

The questionnaire we employed (see Appendix B) was a shortened, modified version of that used in the high-intensity social marketing experiment. The most critical questions contained in the original high-intensity questionnaire were condensed into a one-page, two-sided instrument, soliciting information concerning handbook usage and general reactions, factors presenting obstacles to guideline implementation, and general practitioner demographic data. The low-intensity study instrument, then, paralleled that of the high-intensity study. A discussion of the initial work in developing the utilization questionnaire appears in Appendix C.

The questionnaire attempted to gauge the depth of utilization of the handbook, asking a series of questions that probed small, incremental degrees of use. This ranged from failure to receive or examine the handbook to using it to implement a guideline fully with a resulting high degree of goal attainment. The items, in order of incremental utilization, are as follows:

- I did not receive a copy of the Handbook.
- I received a copy of the Handbook.
- I examined the Handbook
  Read it
  Studied it.
- After examining the Handbook, I later thought about or referred back to it.
- After examining the Handbook, I seriously considered applying it to my practice.
- I applied some of the concepts from the Handbook, either in a formal or informal manner.
- I partially implemented a specific action guideline
  (stopped before completing tasks of implementation)
  Did not use the Handbook in a systematic way
  Used the Handbook in a systematic way.
- I fully implemented a specific action guideline
  Moderately attained the goal (less than 75% attainment)
  Largely attained the goal (75%-100% attainment)

The purpose of this scale was to group practitioners according to level of handbook usage. Three groups of "utilizers" were distinguished and defined as follows:

(1) *Low Utilizers:* Those practitioners who:
   did not receive a handbook (a distribution problem)
   received but did not examine
   examined handbook only
   read handbook only

(2) *Medium Utilizers:* Those practitioners who:

      studied handbook

      examined, later thought about handbook

      considered applying handbook to practice

      applied concepts in a general way

(3) *High Utilizers:* Those practitioners who:

      partially implemented a guideline systematically

      fully implemented a guideline

      fully implemented with high goal attainment

DATA ACQUISITION

Those individuals who were listed on the agency order cards to receive handbooks (2688 in all) became the sample for analyzing *utilization.* In order to determine the degree of utilization, we sent each practitioner the low-intensity questionnaire after a three-month implementation period. We requested him or her to return the questionnaire directly to our office. Included with the questionnaire was a brochure reiterating the specific appeal assigned to that practitioner's agency and a letter describing the questionnaire's purpose. To preserve confidentiality, no individual names were recorded on the questionnaires, though each questionnaire was assigned an agency code number. This was used for identifying the assigned diffusion approach and for correlating responses with agency background data that had been obtained from the NIMH and the FSAA national offices. The data analysis strategy we employed was identical to that used in the dissemination study.

MEASURING UTILIZATION: THE DEPTH OF UTILIZATION RATIO

The data we obtained through our Low, Medium, and High Utilizer grouping procedure are categorical. This affects the data analysis strategy in precisely the same way as it did in the dissemination substudy. Once again, we turned to a combination of a contingency table analysis and a descriptive ratio, which we refer to as the "Depth of Utilization Ratio" (DUR).

The DUR is a measure of the extent to which handbook material was actually used by practitioners. Its more formal definition is the "aggregate utilization score for all respondents exposed to a given diffusion approach relative to the maximum possible aggregate score for that subsample of respondents." The formula we used to calculate this ratio was:

$$\frac{\text{aggregate Depth of Utilization score}}{\text{number of respondents} \times 3 \text{ (maximum utilization score)}} = \text{DUR}$$

This ratio facilitates a descriptive comparison of the amount of utilization resulting from each diffusion approach. The contingency table analysis permits hypothesis testing and significance level determination for possible differences among utilization levels. While we would emphasize that the contingency tables are not a direct test for differences between DURs, there is an obvious relationship in the direction of their findings: *Those diffusion approaches that result in higher utilization levels than expected in the contingency table analysis will likewise attain a higher DUR level.*

In summary, all information collected for analyzing the extent to which the handbook was *used* came from two sources: practitioners' questionnaires reporting their experiences with and reactions to the handbook, and background organizational data concerning the practitioners' agencies. Almost 2700 practitioners were supplied with handbooks. The extent to which they used those handbooks was to be assessed using our Depth of Utilization Ratio.

Analysis of Problems of Implementation and Procedure

The selection of an appropriate form of analysis was complicated by the various types of independent variables that were included in the follow-up questionnaires as these were related to both the low-intensity and high-intensity substudies. We desired the procedures to allow for parallel and comparable analysis across the two studies. In addition to examining depth of utilization in relationship to type of diffusion leadership, we were interested in personal characteristics of participants, their attitudes toward the handbook and the workshop, and factors in their organizational situation that served to facilitate or hinder their implementation of a guideline in the high-intensity study. There were also features of interest within the general design, such as differences among cities, regions, and different individual workshop leaders.

Our data analysis was complex. In its simplest expression, it could be said that we examined each independent variable in relation to the DU score. In the low-intensity study we were primarily interested in the effects of reference group appeal and point of entry, and secondarily interested in personal attributes of practitioners and agency structural variables as related to handbook use.

Having examined various analysis modes,[1] it seemed evident that a contingency table analysis, with its associated statistics (chi square and maximum likelihood, particularly the former), would be the most appropriate main technique for our purposes. This analysis permits hypothesis testing and provides a clear picture concerning the nature of variable relationships. In addition, this particular technique permits the use of the same statistics on all variables, whether nominal, ordinal, or recorded interval data.

To ensure the validity of the chi square and maximum likelihood statistics, which are the principal tests of the null hypothesis, the *expected* frequencies for cells must be considered. This was a problem in the high-intensity substudy, discussion of which begins with Chapter 6. The size of the sample in the low-intensity study we are currently discussing did not generate such problems. Both chi square and maximum likelihood use the same basic assumptions and models for testing the null hypothesis. Results should be, and were in our study, uniformly similar. (To simplify the presentation we will rely mainly on the chi square.) We obtained the value for each statistic with its associated degrees of freedom, accompanied by a significance level. In our analysis we were looking for a significance level of 5 percent (p = .05) or better.

A Final Word

Our primary interest in conducting these two phases of our low-intensity, mass social marketing study was to gain some understanding of the acceptability of mass social marketing efforts to the human service professional community. We were interested in the specific results our research might yield and in the fit between marketing methods and human service delivery systems. The nature of that fit has been revealed in the procedures, brochures, and arrangements described in this chapter.

Low-intensity social marketing carries special problems and special ramifications. Its exploration necessitates the development of new and sometimes unusual perspectives. As with the whole realm of social R&D and its various appendages, social marketing in general and low-intensity social marketing in particular may require a certain measure of suspension of scientific disbelief. We found that commercial and social research orientations could be melded in a productive and cooperative way. This requires the researcher to proceed with openness, intelligence, and a clear vision of his or her own aims and the parameters within which they are operative. Our substantive study findings, perhaps, do not come through as simply as this process observation. It is to these findings that we next direct our attention.

Note

1. With regard to the nature of the data, most of the independent variables were of a nominal or ordinal nature. This is also true of the main dependent variable, DU, as we assumed that intervals on the scale are not necessarily equal. Cell size for each subgroup of the sample was a factor to be considered as well. Some variables have greatly differing numbers of cases per category; for example, "agency respondents" in the high-intensity study had as few as 4 and as many as 25.

With these factors in mind, a number of analytic techniques were considered. Some, such as t-tests, analysis of variance, and other parametric tests were inappropriate because of the interval data requirements. Most nonparametric tests, such as the Kruskal-Wallis, median tests, or two sample, were eliminated because of the relatively few discrete values that most variables, including DU, assumed.

References

Achenbaum, A. R. Market testing: Using the marketplace as a laboratory. In R. Ferber (Ed.), *Handbook of marketing research.* New York: McGraw-Hill, 1974.

Bass, F., King, C., & Pessemier, E. (Eds.). *Applications of the sciences in marketing management.* New York: John Wiley, 1968.

Cox, K. K., & Enis, B. M. *Experimentation for marketing decisions.* Scranton, PA: International Textbook, 1969.

Cox, W. E. An experimental study of promotional behavior in the industrial market. In R. M. Hass (Ed.), *Science, technology and marketing.* Chicago: American Marketing Association, 1966.

DeLozier, M. W. *The marketing communications process.* New York: McGraw-Hill, 1976.

Enis, B. *Marketing principles.* Pacific Palisades, CA: Goodyear, 1974.

Haskins, J. B. *How to evaluate mass communications.* New York: Advertising Research Foundation, 1968.

Jennsen, W. J. Sales effect of TV, radio, and print advertising. *Journal of Advertising Research,* 1966, 6, 2-7.

Kotler, P., & Zaltman, G. Social marketing: An approach to planned social change. *Journal of Marketing,* 1971, 35(3), 3-12.

Kuehnel, T. G., & Eckman, T. A., Jr. *Planning for adoption of innovations: A social learning perspective for dissemination.* Paper prepared for Conference on Planned Change, sponsored by the National Institute of Mental Health and Program Evaluation Resource Center, New Orleans, December 4, 1976.

McCarthy, J. *Basic marketing: A managerial approach* (3rd ed.). Homewood, IL: Irwin, 1968.

Ray, M. L. The present and potential linkages between the microtheoretical notions of behavioral science and the problems of advertising: A proposal for a research system. In H. L. Davis & A. J. Silk (Eds.), *Behavioral and management science in marketing.* New York: John Wiley, 1978.

Rice, R. E., & Rogers, E. M. Reinvention in the innovation process. *Knowledge: Creation, Diffusion, Utilization,* 1980, 1(4), 499-514.

Twerdt, D. W. (Ed.). *Survey and marketing research.* Chicago: American Marketing Association, 1973.

Venkatesen, M., & Holloway, R. J. *An introduction to marketing experimentation.* New York: Macmillan, 1970.

CHAPTER 5

FINDINGS AND CONCLUSIONS ON MASS COMMUNICATIONS SOCIAL MARKETING

A Brief Look Forward

This chapter is organized under four main topical areas: (1) reference group appeals, (2) points of entry, (3) combined appeal/entry strategy, and (4) summary of findings. Within each topic area we present findings of each of our two substudies (dissemination and utilization) separately. These are further subdivided by data for the CMHC system, the FSAA system, and both service systems combined. We will examine personal and organizational factors regarding appeals when we discuss utilization, as a more substantial number of cases and a larger amount of relevant data were available through that substudy.

Introduction

Reports of results in diffusion studies are frequently dismal (see, for example, Glaser & Ross, 1971). In light of this, our use of social marketing methods in a human services diffusion project can be characterized as positive and encouraging. Overall, the number of agencies responding affirmatively (that is, that ordered handbooks) was better than 40 percent of those contacted. The community mental health agencies were more responsive in that almost half (48.4 percent) of those agencies ordered handbooks. The family service agencies' responses were more modest (36.5 percent). In all, almost 2700 handbooks were ordered, with the larger sample of mental health centers

TABLE 5.1   Distribution Response Pattern

	Number of Agencies in Sample	Number Ordering Handbooks	% Ordering Handbooks	Total Handbooks Distributed
Total	595	257	43.2	2688
CMHCs	335	162	48.4	1760
FSAAs	260	95	36.5	928

asking for nearly twice as many as family service agencies. The response pattern is given in Table 5.1.

In addition, the handbook attained substantial application, with slightly more than one-fifth of the respondents reporting a "high" level of utilization. Another third indicated a "medium" level of utilization. If accurately reported, this would seem to be an impressive degree of subsequent actual usage in agency practice settings. The overall reported utilization results are presented in Figure 5.1.

One additional prefatory comment is in order. We had assumed that social marketing is a complex process involving varied types of potential users (by age, professional affiliation, experience, and so on), each of whom might respond differently to alternative diffusion strategies. It is this variation in the market that necessitates the careful and extensive planning and test marketing for purposes of market segmentation commonly employed in top-level commercial advertising firms. One aspect of the study was geared to determining whether, indeed, variegated or general responses would be found in the human service professional market. As the findings will show, variation and complexity (segmentation) rather than uniformity and simplicity (homogeneity) were revealed as characteristic of this market.

Reference Group Appeals

The chart presented in Figure 5.2 provides a summary of the more effective appeals in both service systems for dissemination and for utilization. Our initial hypothesis was that Bureaucratic

			Level of Utilization		
			Low	Medium	High	Total
	Total	Number	466	334	223	1023
		%	45.6	32.6	21.8	100%
Respondents	CMHCs	Number	343	213	148	704
		%	48.7	30.2	21.0	100%
	FSAAs	Number	123	121	75	319
		%	38.6	37.9	23.5	100%

Figure 5.1: Utilization Results

and Professional Appeals would be strong and about equally matched in the CMHC system, and that the Bureaucratic Appeal would be strongest in the FSAA system. We made no distinctions between results for dissemination and utilization. As the chart in Figure 5.2 indicates, the Bureaucratic Appeal was generally effective, and the Community/Client Appeal was generally ineffective. For utilization, Bureaucratic and Professional Appeals were effective and about equally so in CMHCs. Only the Bureaucratic Appeal seemed to have an effect in FSAAs, and this was somewhat marginal. The dissemination pattern was different. The Bureaucratic Appeal appeared to foster distribution in both systems, although in a less pronounced way in the FSAAs. Neither the Professional nor the Community/Client Appeals appeared to have much of an effect on dissemination. With this preview of results, we will enter into a more detailed discussion of findings.

DISSEMINATION SUBSTUDY

CMHCs–Dissemination

The analysis of community mental health agencies' dissemination responses revealed a decrease in effectiveness of appeal

	Dissemination Findings		Utilization Findings	
	CMHCs	FSAAs	CMHCs	FSAAs
Bureaucratic	XX	X	XX	X
Professional			XX	
Community/ Client				

NOTE: XX = a significantly higher score; X = a strong trend toward a higher score.

Figure 5.2: **More Effective Appeals in CMHCs and FSAAs for Dissemination (Ordering Handbooks) and Utilization (Using Handbooks)**

from Bureaucratic to Professional to Community/Client. The level of significance attained from the contingency table analysis (maximum likelihood $p = .04$, chi square $p = .04$) and the Handbook Dissemination Ratios provide descriptive evidence of the differing results. The ratios were:

Appeal:	*Bureaucratic*	*Professional*	*Community/Client*
	.50	.45	.40

We further stratified CMHCs by personal and organizational variables on which data could be obtained to discover any unique agency characteristics that seemed either to increase or to attenuate the effect of the Appeals. The large majority of variables fell into the same pattern (see Section I, Appendix D).

In reviewing the contingency table results and HDR scores for *all* CMHC stratifications, one general trend was suggestive: The largest agencies (as defined by agency expenditures, staff size, and so forth) tended to be especially susceptible to the Bureaucratic Appeal. This is consistent with what we reported above. Only one variable associated with agency size, the number of auxiliary professionals, did not fit this trend. No clear pattern emerged for small CMHCs.

The Professional Appeal in this substudy was not as strong as we had predicted. Hierarchical effects of large agency size exerted an influence in the bureaucratic direction.

FSAAs–Dissemination

A similar trend in the findings, though not statistically significant, held for family service agencies. Overall, as these HDR scores show, the Bureaucratic Appeal yielded the strongest results:

Appeal:	*Bureaucratic*	*Professional*	*Community/Client*
	.37	.30	.28

This lent a measure of support to our hypothesis regarding this service system. The stratification of various agency characteristics revealed that the Bureaucratic Appeal consistently obtained the highest dissemination ratios among FSAAs especially where the FSAAs were large. These trends, however, were likewise not statistically significant.

Both Systems–Dissemination

Not surprisingly, examining CMHCs and FSAAs as a combined group, we found that the "best" results were obtained with the Bureaucratic Appeal. The same pattern emerged overall, showing the same decreasing order of effectiveness: Bureaucratic, then Professional, then Community/Client. The HDR scores for both systems were as follows:

Appeal:	*Bureaucratic*	*Professional*	*Community/Client*
	.45	.38	.34

Stratification provided us with a clearer indication of what agency variables might be especially important. Six variables, all characteristic of large agencies, emerged as statistically significant, a finding consistent with those reported earlier (see Section II, Appendix D).

Results—Interpretation

The implications of these data are that when one is *disseminating* information to any large agency (and, in lieu of evidence to the contrary, to small agencies, as well), a focus on the Bureaucratic Appeal should yield better results than a focus on the Professional Appeal, which, in turn, should yield better results than the Community/Client Appeal.

We had assumed that the Bureaucratic Appeal would be more predominant for FSAAs, with their preponderance of social workers, than for CMHCs, where staffs include some proportion of established professionals (psychologists and psychiatrists). In fact, the Bureaucratic Appeal stood out more clearly for the CMHCs. There, several variables showed statistical significance (at the .05 level or beyond), while only the trend toward greater strength for the Bureaucratic Appeal emerged for the FSAAs. Since community mental health centers are generally larger than family service agencies, this structural variable may explain the results. The structural variable of size, rather than that pertaining to a greater preponderance of established professionals, seemed to have the more powerful effect.

UTILIZATION SUBSTUDY

The second stage of the low-intensity social marketing experiment concerned assessing the extent to which the social product we disseminated, our handbook, was *actually used* by those who received it. Of the 2688 practitioners who were supplied with handbooks, 38 percent (1025) returned questionnaires; 69 percent of those responding (705) were from CMHCs, and 31 percent (320) were from FSAAs. The distribution of responses was expected as a ratio of number of respondents to sample size.

The extent to which the handbooks were used (the Depth of Utilization score) was described by the 3-point scale discussed earlier:

(1) *Low Utilization:*   did not obtain handbook, simply glanced at or read it (46 percent—466 respondents)

(2) *Medium Utilization:* studied, thought about further, considered applying or actually applied the general concepts (33 percent—334 respondents)

(3) *High Utilization:* partially or fully implemented a handbook guideline (22 percent—223 respondents)

Because an arbitrary cutoff date for response was necessarily set, it is possible that the number of respondents who might have scored at the High Utilization level is understated, while those who scored at the Low and Medium levels are overstated.

CMHCs—Utilization

For CMHCs, overall, both the Bureaucratic and Professional Appeals worked equally well, and better than Community/ Client, in encouraging *use* of the handbook by agency practitioners (maximum likelihood p = .03, chi square p = .03), as demonstrated by these utilization ratio scores:

Appeal:	*Bureaucratic*	*Professional*	*Community/Client*
	.59	.59	.55

(We note that, although the Depth of Utilization Ratio [DUR] and Handbook Dissemination Ratio [HDR] scores have a similar appearance, they are in no way related and are not comparable.)

Stratification, based upon practitioner demographic data and the characteristics of the agency in which the practitioner was employed, resulted in a number of instances of statistical significance. In the majority of these cases the Professional Appeal encouraged the greatest utilization. The exception is for professionals with lower levels of training or fewer years of professional experience (see Section III, Appendix D).

The utilization findings are consistent with our original hypotheses for this system: that the Bureaucratic and Professional Appeals would be strong and coequal (with perhaps a margin of advantage in favor of the Professional).

Using significant results and examining all ratios for trends leads us to a number of conclusions. First, in general, either the

Bureaucratic or Professional Appeal will obtain approximately the same amount of utilization in CMHCs. In addition, with few exceptions, the Community/Client Appeal is the least effective and probably should be underplayed as a tool of persuasion. Respondents who are least experienced in the human service field (holding lower degrees and/or having served relatively few years in the field) seem most encouraged to use the handbook when the Bureaucratic Appeal is used. Those with more experience and higher degrees are most responsive to the Professional Appeal.

FSAAs—Utilization

For FSAAs, the Bureaucratic Appeal appeared to do somewhat better than either the Professional or Community/Client, although not at a statistically significant level (maximum likelihood $p = .32$, chi square $p = .32$):

Appeal:	Bureaucratic	Professional	Community/Client
	.61	.59	.59

There is no clear differentiation between the Professional and Community/Client Appeals; both worked about the same.

Both Systems—Utilization

The results for both systems are not statistically significant. The trend that emerges, however, suggests that the Bureaucratic Appeal may be preferred over the Professional, which in turn appeals to be stronger than the Community/Client.

As FSAA respondents were receptive to the Bureaucratic Appeal, while CMHC respondents were clearly equally receptive to either the Bureaucratic or Professional Appeals, one might expect that combining the two systems would produce a leaning somewhat in the direction of the Bureaucratic Appeal. This appeared to occur (maximum likelihood $p = .08$, chi square $p = .07$), as the utilization ratio scores for both systems show:

Appeal:	Bureaucratic	Professional	Community/Client
	.61	.59	.56

When stratifying the sample by practitioner and agency characteristics, most instances of statistical significance (with one exception) showed the Bureaucratic Appeal as having the highest DURs (see Section IV, Appendix D). These stratified results appear to lead to the conclusion that the Bureaucratic Appeal influenced subgroups of respondents consistently to use the material to a higher degree than either of the other two appeals. The Community/Client Appeal was least important once again as an influencer of behavior. If faced with directing a single message to members of both service systems, the Bureaucratic Appeal would appear to offer the best potential for encouraging *utilization.*

Point of Entry

We had hypothesized that there would be no significant differences among the various points of entry used in the design. This position was based in part on the theoretical formulation of Litwak et al. (1970) concerning "human relations" agency structures. The hypothesis was substantially confirmed. There were no significant differences in the dependent variable measures among the three channels into the organization. Point of entry, apparently, whether Executive, Training Specialist, or Special Interest person, was not a significant factor in the dissemination of the handbook; neither was it a significant factor in determining the extent of its utilization within the system.

There was one sample subset, *Practitioners with a Social Work Identification,* that yielded significant differences in Depth of Utilization results:

Entry:	*Executive*	*Trainer*	*Special Interest*	*Chi Square*
	.652	.575	.661	p = .03

Those with a social work identification were more likely to implement guidelines when either the Executive or Special Interest Entry points were used. The Training Entry was not useful for encouraging guideline implementation.

Briefly, we can chart our results of these analyses as follows:

Service System	Entry
All Respondents	No significance overall for different entry points. For practitioners with a Social Work identification, the Training Entry was marginally less effective.
CMHC Respondents	Entry point was not a significant factor. No CMHC DURs appeared to be affected by Entry point.
FSAA Respondents	No significant differences for different points of entry. Either the Executive or Special Interest worked marginally better than the Training Entry. This was especially true for respondents from large FSAA agencies (FSAA agencies have a preponderance of social work professionals).

The hypothesis of equivalency of entry points was largely confirmed. In addition to the human relations structural theory, these equivalency results may be explained in two additional ways—one substantive, the other methodological.

We might assume (contrary to the Litwak position) that executives have a measure of influence in the organization but are assailed by many inputs into the organization and have a wide range of issues that concern them. A matter dealing with training or with some aspects of community outreach may not be of special importance to them compared, for example, to questions of budget, federal regulations, or board pressures. If a particular innovation does happen to attract their attention, however, they can exert much influence in steering the innovation through the agency.

The Training and Special Interest people do not typically have strong hierarchical influence in the organization. However, the handbrook may nevertheless be of special saliency to them in terms of training or operational responsibilities. They may be more likely to have their attention drawn to the handbook but have less influence than the director in steering it through the agency. These attributes may cancel each other out so that an equivalent level of impact is reached.

The other interpretation reflects on the methods of the study. Mailings were addressed to "Executive Director," "Training Specialist," and "Consultation and Education Specialist" or "Family Advocate." There may be considerable variation within agencies regarding the existence of the positions other than the Executive. In smaller agencies (FSAAs) especially, the full range of roles may not exist. In those cases the communication may have been directed to the Executive or to a substitute staff person, selected by a secretary or receptionist. This may also have caused the findings to be canceled out.

We are persuaded that if the same procedures as employed in the study were used in actual agency dissemination work (that is, sending innovative materials to formal, titled positions in agencies without having detailed information about the aggregation of receivers and agency positional structure), the result would have been the same as in this instance. There would be about equal usage, regardless of which titled position one used for disseminating materials. It makes no difference, in other words, which point-of-entry titled position is used.

Our findings do not relate to another set of circumstances: where each of these titled positions in the agency is known to exist and/or the actual name of the position occupant is identified and the communication is addressed to that position or person. Further, our findings do not deal at all with methods in which each of these known point-of-entry position occupants are approached in a direct, personal way (high intensity) by a dissemination agent.

Combined Appeal/Entry Strategy

In this subanalysis we examined the interaction between Entry and Appeal with respect to diffusion activities. It seemed logical that Executives would respond best to the Bureaucratic Appeal, the Training Person to the Professional Appeal, and the Special Interest person to the Community/Client Appeal.

The data did not support our assumptions. While the Special Interest Person gave a slight indication of being influenced by the Community/Client Appeal (though more influenced by the Bureaucratic Appeal), on the whole we were forced to conclude that, for this sample at least, Entry-Appeal interactions were of trivial consideration in formulating Entry-Appeal strategies. Combined strategy HDR scores for both systems were as follows:

	Bureaucratic	Professional	Community/Client
Executive	.42	.43	.29
Training	.47	.38	.34
Special Interest	.44	.38	.40

Summary:
Effects of Appeal and Entry
on Dissemination and Utilization

APPEAL

Many variables were analyzed with varying results for the different substudies and delivery systems. To reiterate, we have reasonable confidence that a Bureaucratic Appeal will facilitate *dissemination* and *utilization* of new practice tools in agencies similar to those to whom we directed our attention (the effect was less pronounced for FSAAs than for CMHCs). A *Professional Appeal* is more delimited in effect; that is, it seems to facilitate *utilization,* but *not necessarily dissemination,* and it operated in that fashion on only one of the two service delivery systems (CMHCs). *Community/Client Appeals* seem to be *ineffective* in accomplishing either purpose.

Appeal appears to be a highly complex variable, revealing differences among the two different delivery systems in our research and for dissemination as compared to utilization.

The following personal and organizational influences appear to be at work in *utilization* responses to different appeals:

- *Age:* older staff responsive to Professional Appeal
  younger staff responsive to Bureaucratic Appeal
  neither responsive to Community/Client Appeal
- *Gender:* no variations in responses to Appeals among males and females
- *Education:* more educated staff responsive to Professional Appeal
  less educated staff responsive to Bureaucratic Appeal
  neither responsive to Community/Client Appeal
- *Experience:* more experienced staff responsive to Professional Appeal
  less experienced staff responsive to Bureaucratic Appeal
  neither responsive to Community/Client Appeal
- *Agency Size:* staff in larger agencies responsive to *both* Professional and Bureaucratic Appeals
  staff in smaller agencies responsive to Bureaucratic Appeal
  staff in neither responsive to Community/Client Appeal

Certain types of agencies that we felt would be especially responsive to Community/Client Appeals did not manifest such response patterns. This included those with larger proportions of minority staff and nongraduate social workers and those with small populations to serve. Agencies with larger numbers of staff in auxiliary organizational maintenance roles were especially responsive to Bureaucratic Appeals.

We find the pervasive low level of response by agency staff to Community/Client Appeals striking and perhaps disturbing. Whether this is due to recruitment, training, socialization, or other factors is unanswerable through this study. It does, however, suggest a different order of problem to be looked into.

ENTRY

Overall, there were no significant variations using different agency points of entry. Figure 5.3 reviews those tendencies, of a nonsignificant nature, that we were able to identify.

In spite of the general weakness of Entry as a discriminating factor, we were able to note a few marginal trends. The Executive and Special Interest Entries were somewhat favored in the FSAAs for both types of social marketing. In FSAAs we found that the Trainer Entry was particularly ineffective, regardless of the size of the agency. The Trainer Entry was slightly favored in CMHCs, but only in relation to dissemination. It had no effect on utilization in either service system, contrary to what one might expect.

Entry, then, was a weak discriminating factor with respect to different modes of diffusion. It need not be a critical strategic variable to plan for in designing a social marketing campaign, as other variables will, perhaps, offer greater outcome leverage.

COMBINED STRATEGY

We believed originally that the Bureaucratic, Professional, and Community/Client Appeals would probably be most effective when combined with the Executive, Training, and Special Interest Entries, respectively, forming a diagonal pattern across the nine-cell design diagram. This combined approach, however, was not an operative factor in the dissemination and utilization of the handbook. The speculation/hypothesis was not substantiated. Very likely, this was because the Entry variable was not strongly associated with differential diffusion rates among our study agencies. Generally, Bureaucratic Appeals were better, regardless of Entry, and Community/Client Appeals were weaker, regardless of Entry.

	Dissemination		Utilization		Conclusions
	CMHCs	FSAAs	CMHCs	FSAAs	
Executive		X		X	No significant differences for different entries. The Executive was not an effective Entry point for CMHCs and staff. Slight trends were noticed that the Executive (and Special Interest) Entries were effective for encouraging dissemination and utilization in the FSAA system.
Training	X				No significant differences for different entries. The director of staff training was generally ineffective in promoting dissemination and utilization. There was a slight trend in CMHCs that implied that the training director would be an effective means of distributing innovative material. The worst results, however, in FSAAs were obtained when using the Training Entry.
Special Interest		X		X	No significant differences for different entries. The Special Interest Entry obtained results similar to the Executive. For dissemination in CMHCs, the Special Interest Entry obtained results between the more favorable Training and less favorable Executive. CMHC utilization results were comparable for each Entry used. Slight trends for FSAAs showed the Special Interest Entry (and Executive) to obtain better dissemination and utilization results.

NOTE: X = trend.

Figure 5.3: Summary of Entry Effects

119

Conclusion

Perhaps a principal finding of this low-intensity social marketing study is that variables such as those we examined are factors to be considered in the social marketing process, and that they operate in complex and sometimes unpredictable ways. Our limited research persuades us that the dynamics of communication within and among human services systems are not well understood. Such variables, it appears, are salient in designing a campaign for the dissemination and subsequent utilization of innovative practice tools. The experience of marketers in the realm of commercial enterprise strongly suggests that there are others that should be explored and exploited. In the human service sphere, for example, we have little real concept of the costs of information dissemination, except to know that they are constantly rising. We at present lack the capability of describing social markets with precision and targeting them with effect. Such an approach would require the same kind of rigor and attention in diffusing research-derived products as in designing and conducting the original research itself.

This would involve analytical functions, such as diagnosing the relevant system, delineating different target populations, identifying the characteristics and response patterns of these populations, and designing differential and well-articulated dissemination programs for each target group. We would hope that the knowledge base for accomplishing this effectively will evolve as the recognition of the importance of proper diffusion crystallizes in the human service fields. Meanwhile, we turn our attention to a substantially different form of social marketing, the high-intensity, personal contact approach. We were interested in the relative impact of this alternative mode of diffusion and in the different dynamics that would be at work.

References

Glaser, E. M., & Ross, H. L. *Increasing the utilization of applied research results* (final report to the National Institute of Mental Health). Los Angeles: Human Interaction Institute, 1971.

Litwak, E., Figueira-McDonough, J., Agemian, J., Hamilton, G., & Rhoades, G. *Towards the multi-factor theory and practice of linkages between formal organizations.* Washington, DC: Social and Rehabilitation Services Department, U.S. Department of Health, Education and Welfare, 1970.

PART III

AN INTERPERSONAL APPROACH TO SOCIAL MARKETING

CHAPTER 6
ISSUES IN INTERPERSONAL SOCIAL MARKETING

A Brief Look Forward

In this chapter we present the second of our two social marketing substudies. This "high-intensity" study is concerned with methods of diffusion that employ direct, interpersonal contact as a mode of communication and influence. We give special attention to different types of diffusion agents operating in person in the human service agency setting. We examine the theoretical advantages and disadvantages of the diffusion agent's indigenous or exogenous relationship to the target agency and of the agent's superordinate or peer status in relation to others in the agency.

Introduction

Despite extensive research and theoretical exposition, a number of issues concerning diffusion and/or change agents remain clouded and in dispute. Considerable controversy surrounds two factors in particular that relate to the attributes of the diffusion agent: The agent's relationship to a target agency, and the agent's status in that target agency. The first of these concerns whether or not the diffusion agent should be indigenous to the system selected for the diffusion effort or enter as an outsider. The second concerns whether the diffusion agent should have superordinate status in the agency targeted for the diffusion or have more of a peer relationship with the preponderant number of users in that agency. Available social science literature on these matters is more useful in generating ideas and delineating problems than it is in offering conclusions. Marketing theory is no better in offering us definitive answers.

Marketing scholars subsume direct-contact agent issues under the rubric of "personal selling." Enis and Chonko (1978, p. 280) conceptualize the area as representing an interpersonal transaction wherein the agent and salesperson "is the catalyst for exchange processes." In this exchange, according to DeLozier (1976, p. 81), a general communication principle can be expressed to the effect that "people tend to be influenced by others much like themselves." In more specific marketing terms: "Perceived similarity between the sales representative and his prospect can enhance communications interaction and the probability of a sale" (DeLozier, 1976, p. 250). According to Robertson (1978), people normally associate with individuals who hold similar beliefs and attitudes; and influence tends to be exchanged among individuals of like social status and backgrounds. Accordingly, a useful marketing strategy is to employ a "conscious policy of matching salesman and customer characteristics" (Robertson, 1978, p. 23). Research support for this view has been offered in sales areas such as paints (Brock, 1965), music equipment (Woodside & Davenport, 1974), insurance (Gadel, 1964), and others. A recent review of research on personal selling can be found in Churchill et al. (1981).

Relating these marketing notions to the issues in this study, one would assume that the internal agents and peers have characteristics that are more "homophylous" to the target user group than those of the external and authority agents. Hence, it might be predicted that internal and peer situations would likely bring about higher rates of diffusion. This, however, needs to be placed in an "all other things being equal" context. For example, an agency executive may have little social compatability or interpersonal attraction at his or her disposal, but may command power, resources, and legitimation that will compensate for that deficit. Likewise, the external expert may possess luster and prestige that more than offset the individual's dissimilarity from a target group. Indeed, that person's recognized distinctiveness among professionals may be the very thing that makes for his or her effectiveness as a diffusion agent. It is no surprise, then, that when reviewing a broad range of marketing research on this subject, Hollander (1978, p. 95) was led to conclude that "the question of whether salespeople should be similar to their customer remains perplexing and intriguing."

An examination of diffusion literature gives us a closer view of some key issues to be considered in this area.

Internal Versus External Diffusion Agents

The literature is divided concerning whether the internal person or the external person is more apt to be a successful change agent. The controversy has existed for years. Havelock (1970, p. 47) states:

> Change agents have long debated the relative advantages of beginning as an insider or as an outsider. When all the pros and cons are tallied, however, neither position seems to be clearly superior.

Various organizational elements may affect innovation adoption rates. Corwin (1974) suggests that the quality of linkage between internal and external components of the organizational system, its ability to filter and mediate external stimuli, and the nature of boundary personnel are all significant determinants of an organization's predisposition to adopt innovations. In his view, both internal and external organizational factors are involved in the issue. The arguments surrounding this question point up favorable features of internally and externally directed change; we will review these in turn.

ADVANTAGES OF THE INTERNAL AGENT

The internal person is familiar with the organization, its goals and objectives, its communication channels, its aspirations, its informal centers of power, its resources, and the personality traits of its members. The importance of such familiarity is pointed out by Havelock (1970) and Jenks (1973). Watson and Glaser (1965) concur, suggesting that the internal change agent has the advantages of knowing the programs, its problems, its strengths (which are sometimes hidden), and its potential and actual resources. Havelock and Havelock (1973) also support the importance of familiarity and speak of the difficulty outside agents have in "getting inside the skin" of the organization.

The organization is in turn familiar with the internal change agent. It knows of that person's past experiences, personality, and way of doing things. Therefore, the system and its members may be put more at ease by an insider than by an outsider. The insider is established as an associate. There is already a basis for being accepted by the staff. The insider's values and beliefs are known. The internal change agent is not viewed as an uniformed, demanding stranger. Such an individual commands and gives a certain amount of security and visibility. Colleagues may call on the inside change agent, solicit opinions, request explanations, or ask for more in-depth discussions of the innovation without feeling as uncomfortable as they might with an outsider. Paul (1977, p. 39) puts it this way:

> Legitimacy helps to explain why teachers seem to work well with one another, viz., mutual legitimacy and concomitant credibility, trust and shared values. . . . [They] may be suspicious of outside agents entering the system with ready made solutions.

Havelock and Havelock (1973, p. 42) state:

> Everyone needs a home-base and a colleague system to provide security, identity, visibility, and the kinds of accouterments that are generally required for role maintenance over an extended time period.

A time dimension may be at play here—the insider remains present on an ongoing basis to prove and reinforce the staff continually in regard to the innovative techniques and ideas. The internal person can provide this day-by-day visibility and availability and can identify with the organization more readily. Such a person is both familiar with the organization and can internalize its goals, norms, and aspirations. Havelock and Havelock (1973, p. 29) speak of the difficulty outsiders have in "truly identifying with the client." This social psychological assimilation can be crucial to change agent success, and the insider begins here with an advantage. Campbell (1974) holds that because of lack of familiarity, the external change is more apt to be a source of dysfunctional conflict and organizational demoralization.

The insider generally has more knowledge of, and the ability to use, community resources that are important to his or her agency. Havelock (1970) contends that the insider is more apt to make positive contact with community leaders and innovators to gain community support. The outsider must gain perspective of particular agency-specific community resources over some extended period of time. Research by Van deVall and Bolas (1981) and Bursk and Sethi (1975) found specific empirical support for internal agent advantage.

The insider, then, offers these major advantages as a diffusion agent: (1) a knowledge of the workings of the organization; (2) familiarity with the staff being influenced; (3) a knowledge of the agency's "language"; (4) long-term, day-to-day contact and visibility; (5) the likelihood of easy identification with the system; and (6) likely knowledge and facility in the use of community resources and community people.

ADVANTAGES OF THE EXTERNAL AGENT

The external person offers a new outlook. Havelock (1970, pp. 47-50) states: "[The outsider] starts fresh . . . [and] is in a position to have perspective . . . to bring in something genuinely new." Watson and Glaser (1965) also support the view that the outside consultant (change agent) offers perspective ("a fresh start"). Griffiths (1964) contends that the major impetus for organizational change *must* come from the outside, and much of this is based on the new perspective offered by the outside change agent. Corwin (1974, p. 713) found that organizational innovation is significantly associated with the efforts of an "outside organization staffed by competent and liberal members." A new perspective has important ramifications: It can provide a spark to an otherwise dormant change process; it can provide excitement, a sense of drama; and it can nurture an incentive to change, improve, and modify organizational function. Gordon and Rubenstein (1975) provide illustrative case documentation.

The outsider is able to approach the organization in an objective and independent manner. The outsider has no vested interests within the organization or any identification with partisan factions. Seashore and Van Egmond (1966) and Gross et al. (1971) address the effectiveness growing out of such objectivity. French and Bell (1973) suggest that this position permits greater risk taking on the part of the change agent in fostering innovation. Watson and Glaser (1965) contend that the outside person stands apart from the organizational power structure and possesses energy that is not usurped by ongoing organizational duties. These authors contend that by being independent, disinterested, and focused primarily on the change process, the external change agent can be more effective.

The outsider has an aura of expertise that commands respect. Fairweather et al. (1974) believe that the outside change agent's leadership role is of critical importance. This leadership is, of course, predominantly dependent upon legitimation derived from expertise and prestige. Havelock (1970) asserts that one of the major virtues of the external change agent is unique, specialized skill. Watson and Glaser (1965, p. 36) state: "The outside advisor may be variously viewed as a trouble-maker, as a *knowledgeable specialist,* or as a helpful friend." All in all, an external person offers special competencies and experience. The outsider is in a position to command respect based on reputation, specialized knowledge, and the climate of expectation that may surround him or her.

The outsider can sometimes gain acceptance in the organization more easily as a result of lack of identification with established organizational roles. Havelock and Havelock (1973, p. 42) state:

> The change agent can often be more effective as an "outsider" than as an "insider" partly because of the great difficulties in gaining acceptance for a new role in an old system with long-established traditions.

The external person is not burdened by established stereotypes (Watson & Glaser, 1965). While the insider may need to expend energy and resources competing with the fixed conceptions of the agency, the outsider can proceed immediately to the job at hand. In this instance it is not the outsider's objectivity per se, but an apparent detachment from existing organizational categories or functions that stands him or her in good stead.

The outsider, then: (1) offers new perspective, drama, and excitement; (2) has the potential to be objective, independent, and free of conflicting roles/interests; (3) may be viewed as an expert who commands respect; and (4) has flexibility and scope because of the absence of stereotypic staff impressions that may impede the insider.

A persuasive case can be made for either the insider or the outsider as a diffusion agent. Lippitt et al. (1958, p. 134), in their classic work, put it this way:

> Often the client system seems to be seeking assurance that the potential change agent is different enough from the client system to be a real expert and yet enough like it to be thoroughly understandable and approachable.

Which of these predilections is of greater moment remains an open question. More recently, Paul (1977, p. 38) has stated the issue as follows: "External change agents may bring about greater awareness of innovation and change, but they must overcome resistance."

The insider may have less social distance to bridge but may lack legitimation as a change force. It appears to be a "checks and balances" phenomenon. The same kinds of crosscurrents and uncertainties pertain to authority versus peer status in a diffusion agent.

Authority Versus Peer Diffusion Agents

There has been substantial debate on the positive and negative aspects of authority versus peer influence, with neither approach emerging as clearly superior. Terms such as "power," "coercion," "familiarity," "opinion leadership," and so forth come into play in considering the question of who would make a better change agent, an authority figure or a peer. We will first examine those attributes of the peer person that favor him or her as a change agent.

ADVANTAGES OF THE PEER AGENT

The peer relates to organization members on an informal, familiar basis. The peer's lack of formal rank or authority facilitates easier interactive communication. Havelock and Havelock (1973, p. 20) comment, "Informal person-to-person contact is an important factor in effective dissemination." Palumbo (1969) also indicates that the more formalized an organization, the less likely it is to be innovative. Rothman (1974, p. 462) states, "The innovativeness of an organization is inversely related to the organization's degree of formalization." Rogers and Shoemaker (1971) contend that the peer change agent is able to communicate well with the staff because the peer is more "homophylous" or like those who are the targets of change. There are fewer status or system culture differences involved, and communication is more likely to be smooth.

The peer change agent ordinarily knows staff problems, tasks, and personalities more intimately than the authority person. Havelock and Havelock (1973, p. 20) state, "Effective dissemination and utilization are facilitated by informal opinion leaders." The literature suggests that informal opinion leaders gain their status by being familiar with, and by being in a position to be responsive to, line personnel. This knowledge allows peer change agents to mold and modify themselves, the programs, or their target groups to facilitate the adoption of an innovation. The executive is removed from such on-the-line information, as indicated by Watson and Glaser (1965, p. 36):

> When a top management man takes the lead in making changes, he . . . runs risks. He depends on others in his organization to keep him informed—before, during, and after the change process. But he may only get the kind of feedback his subordinates think he wants to hear, for no one wants to be the bearer of ill tidings to his boss . . . he may incur resistance or even sabotage.

A peer agent does not exert the pressure of coercion that can be brought to bear by an authority change agent. Absence of coercive power eliminates the need for defensiveness and resistance. Hage and Dewar (1971) found that hierarchy of authority was negatively related to program innovation. Griffiths (1964) likewise notes that hierarchy of authority inhibits organizational change. These authors point to the coercion exerted by the authority figure and suggest that peer-initiated change is more likely to gain acceptance, partly because the peer change agent is "one of us."

The peer as change agent permits the staff to identify with the innovation, to see it as their own, and, as a result, to take more energetic responsibility in carrying out the necessary activities. This interaction of one equal with another can foster a sense of personal involvement with the innovation. Palumbo (1969), Hage and Dewar (1971), and Griffiths (1964) all support the view that peer-initiated change fosters participation and increases identification with an innovation. Havelock (1969, p. 35) states, "Decentralization offers increased capacity for knowledge flow and utilization."

Peer-initiated change can lead to better communication flow. Katz and Kahn (1966, p. 246) comment:

> The more top heavy the organization structure and the more control which is exercised through pressures and sanctions, the less adequate will be the flow of information up the line.

Wilensky (1967) notes that for each hierarchical level, there is a probability of misrepresentation and concealment of information. It is contended that as the number of levels through which communication flows to the implementing staff is reduced, the greater the likelihood of accuracy of information, openness, and eventual adoption of an innovation. Generally speaking, the advantages of the peer agent can be summarized as follows: (1) informal relationships with coworkers; (2) enhanced communication; (3) organizational knowledge and familiarity; (4) on-the-line knowledge and adaptability; and (5) a sense of oneness with the staff as an equal.

ADVANTAGES OF THE AUTHORITY AGENT

It would appear from this discussion that logic favors the peer change agent. There are factors, however, that favor the authority change agent. The authority change agent commands power, force, and/or formal authority. Corwin (1974) observes that centralization is positively related to scores of innovation. Rogers and Shoemaker (1971) enumerate several generalizations regarding aspects of behavior that can facilitate an authority-initiated innovation. Paul (1977, p. 40) indicates that in instituting a new program, "hierarchical support can be critical"; he elaborates:

> Although teachers work well with fellow teachers, their efforts may prove insufficient unless hierarchical support is provided. In other words, formal authority may be needed to legitimize teacher efforts, to provide resources and to furnish necessary coordinating activities.

The authority change agent may be more *efficient* in initiating change. Rogers and Shoemaker (1971) and Zaltman et al. (1973) indicate that the speed of authority-initiated change may be advantageous compared with peer change. Both sources observe that optimal decisions made by authority can be made more rapidly than the "collective" type (those made by peers). Zaltman et al. (1973, pp. 80-81) state:

> Decision by authority is usually regarded as efficient because of the sequencing through the subphases of the initiation stage, and thus

the implementation decision can be made within a relatively short period of time.

The contention here is that speed will lead to higher rates of adoption. This is a result of the lack of need for involving all concerned parties in considerations of the alternatives in order to arrive at a consensual agreement.

The authority change agent normally commands an important measure of prestige. The presumption is that authority inherently carries an aura of respect and legitimation. Becker (1970) states that an organization with a chief executive who keeps up with recent trends in the profession is more likely to adopt innovations due to the prestige commanded by the authority figure. Carlson (1965) also speaks to this issue of prestige, noting that the individual who commands prestige as a result of both position and skills is more likely to be a successful innovator.

The authority change agent occupies a critical position in, and control over, the communication networks within the organization and between the organization and outside systems. Becker (1970) and Carlson (1965) suggest that the executive who is centrally located in the communication network has enormous control over the amount and direction of communication within the organization. Such an individual, therefore, can be extremely effective in steering change. There are, however, antecedent conditions that precede the implementation of any change process. The change agent must first be persuaded of, or "sold on," the need for particular change. We may summarize the advantages of the authority diffusion agent as follows: (1) power, formal authority; (2) legitimation; (3) speed of implementation; (4) prestige; and (5) critical location at the center of the communication network.

A Multiple-Contingency Approach

Because of the unsettled, open-ended state of knowledge in these areas, we proceeded in an exploratory manner in our social marketing studies. In our high-intensity, personal contact work, we examined these issues in a direct and systematic way, but without proffering specific hypotheses that were intended, ultimately, to predict relationships among variables. Rather, we engaged in a more fluid type of relationship testing. At the same time, we were on the lookout for contingent variables that might explain conditions under which one or another of these approaches might be differentially more effective in diffusing innovations.

The pattern reflected in the literature suggests that categorical, ubiquitous hypotheses may not be helpful. Instead, more refined approaches, describing circumstances under which one or another approach might bring about better results, would appear to be a way of bringing greater enlightenment to the discussion. Our social marketing studies allow for the emergence of such explanatory contingencies through the inclusion of a wide range of variables within their respective designs. This is consistent with certain current approaches in the marketing field. Hofer (1975), for example, suggests a "contingency theory of business strategy" whereby cause-effect relationships among variables are isolated gradually in order to generate strategic propositions. Commenting on this, Boyd and Larreche (1978, p. 64) state:

> There are obviously problems in the building of such a contingency theory because of the sheer number of situations and lack of empirical evidence. . . . Additional field research, however, should make this approach more feasible in the future.

In the next chapter we will describe the field research design of this particular social marketing undertaking, which was aimed at formulating such strategic guidelines.

References

Becker, M. Sociometric location and innovativeness: Reformation and extension of the diffusion model. *American Sociological Review*, 1970, 35(2), 267-282.

Boyd, H. W., Jr., & Larreche, J.-C. The foundations of marketing strategy. In G. Zaltman & T. V. Bonoma (Eds.), *Review of marketing 1978*. Pittsburgh: Co-sponsored by the American Marketing Association, the Marketing Science Institute, and the Graduate School of Business, 1978.

Brock, T. C. Communicator-Recipient Similarity and decision change. *Journal of Personality and Social Psychology,* 1965, 1, 650-654.

Bursk, E. C., & Sethi, B. S. *The in-house advertising agency.* Unpublished manuscript, 1975.

Campbell, D. T. *Assessing the impact of planned social change.* Paper presented at the OECD Seminar on Social Research and Public Policies, Dartmouth, September 13-15, 1974.

Carlson, R. O. *Adoption of educational innovations.* Eugene: Center for the Advanced Study of Educational Administration, University of Oregon, 1965.

Churchill, G. A., Jr., et al. *Sales force management: Planning, implementation and control.* Homewood, IL: Irwin, 1981.

Corwin, R. C. Strategies for organizational innovation. In Y. Hasenfeld & R. A. English (Eds.) *Human service organizations.* Ann Arbor: University of Michigan Press, 1974.

DeLozier, M. W. *The marketing communications process.* New York: McGraw-Hill, 1976.

Enis, B. M., & Chonko, L. B. A review of personal selling: Implications for managers and researchers. In G. Zaltman & T. V. Bonoma (Eds.), *Review of marketing 1978.* Pittsburgh: Cosponsored by the American Marketing Association, the Marketing Science Institute, and the Graduate School of Business, 1978.

Fairweather, G. W., Sanders, D. H., & Tornatzky, L. G. *Creating change in mental health organizations.* New York: Pergamon, 1974.

French, W. L., & Bell, C. H. *Organizational development.* Englewood Cliffs, NJ: Prentice-Hall, 1973.

Gadel, M. S. Concentration by salesman on congenial prospects. *Journal of Marketing,* 1964, 28, 64-66.

Gordon, B. R., & Rubenstein, D. I. The socially constructive aspects of outside agents in community decision-making in a rural area. *Journal of Sociology and Social Welfare,* 1975, 2(4), 451-459.

Griffiths, D. E. Administrative theory and change in organizations. In M. B. Miles (Ed.), *Innovation in education.* New York: Bureau of Publications, Teachers College, Columbia University, 1964.

Gross, N. J., Giaequinta, J. B. & Bernstein, M. *Implementing organizational innovations.* New York: Basic Books, 1971.

Hage, J., & Dewar, R. *The prediction of organizational performance: The case of program innovation.* Paper presented at the American Sociological Association annual meetings, Denver, Colorado, August 1971.

Havelock, R. G. *Planning for innovation through dissemination and utilization of scientific knowledge.* Ann Arbor: University of Michigan, 1969.

Havelock, R. G. *A guide to innovation in education.* Ann Arbor: Center for Research on the Utilization of Scientific Knowledge, Institute for Social Research, University of Michigan, 1970.

Havelock, R. G., & Havelock, M. C. *Training for change agents.* Ann Arbor: Center for Research on the Utilization of Scientific Knowledge, Institute for Social Research, University of Michigan, 1973.

Hofer, C. W. Toward a contingency theory of business strategy. *Academy of Management Journal,* 1975, 18(4), 784-810.

Hollander, S. C. Retailing research. In G. Zaltman & T. V. Bonoma (Eds.), *Review of marketing 1978.* Pittsburgh: Cosponsored by the American Marketing Association, the Marketing Science Institute, and the Graduate School of Business, 1978.

Jenks, R. S. An internal change agent's role in restructuring university governance. *Journal of Higher Education,* 1973, 44(5), 370-379.

Katz, D., & Kahn, R. L. *The social psychology of organizations.* New York: John Wiley, 1966.

Lippitt, R., Watson, J., & Westley, B. *The dynamics of planned change.* New York: Harcourt Brace Jovanovich, 1958.

Palumbo, D. J. Power and role specificity in organizational theory. *Public Administration Review,* 1969, 29(3), 237-248.

Paul, D. A. Change processes at the elementary, secondary and post-secondary levels of education. In N. Nash & J. Culbertson (Eds.), *Linking processes in educational improvement: Concepts and applications.* Columbus, OH: University Council for Educational Administration, 1977.

Robertson, T. S. Diffusion theory and the concept of personal influence. In H. L. Davis & A. J. Silk (Eds.), *Behavioral and management science in marketing.* New York: John Wiley, 1978.

Rogers, E. M., & Shoemaker, F. F. *Communication of innovations: A cross cultural approach.* New York: Macmillan, 1971.

Rothman, J. *Planning and organizing for social change: Action principles from social science research.* New York: Columbia University Press, 1974.

Seashore, C., Van Egmond, E. The consultant-trainer role. In W. Bennis et al. (Eds.), *The planning of change.* New York: Holt, Rinehart & Winston, 1966.

Van deVall, M., & Bolas, C. External vs. internal social policy researchers. *Knowledge: Creation, Diffusion, Utilization,* 1981, 2(4), 461-481.

Watson, G., & Glaser, E. M. What we have learned about planning for change. *Management Review,* 1965, 54(11), 34-46.

Wilensky, H. *Organizational intelligence.* New York: Basic Books, 1967.

Woodside, A. G., & Davenport, J. W. The effect of salesman similarity and expertise on consumer purchasing behavior. *Journal of Marketing Research,* 1974, 11, 198-202.

Zaltman, G., Duncan, R., Holbek, J. *Innovations and organizations.* New York: John Wiley, 1973.

CHAPTER 7

STUDYING INTERPERSONAL SOCIAL MARKETING

A Brief Look Forward

We begin this chapter with a succinct review of the objectives and general design of the high-intensity substudy. The participating agencies in the sample are described and the sampling procedure is discussed. The instrument for measuring utilization is indicated, and the rationale for the approach taken to measurement is placed in context. We show the interrelation between use of a workshop diffusion medium and the use of an in-person, on-the-scene diffusion agent, including some of the complexities included in determining the appropriate mode of influence to be studied under the circumstances. We conclude with a discussion of our data analysis procedures.

Introduction

In this social marketing study, once again, the innovation to be disseminated was a handbook conveying two community-oriented intervention techniques or, as we called them, "Action Guidelines." These guidelines were research-based and reliably tested tools to be used by mental health professionals. One consisted of procedures for increasing participation; the other, for promoting new services and programs. The same two service systems, community mental health centers and family service agencies, were selected as our target market segments in this substudy.

Two external and two internal personal interaction diffusion agents were used to disseminate the handbook. They employed, primarily, a workshop medium for communicating with their target market. The agents represented a direct contact or "personal sales" approach to marketing an innovative product. Workshops were conducted in 37 different agencies in 8 different cities.

Within each of these approaches authority and peer agents were used. Internal authority agents were members of the executive staff of the agency. Internal peer agents were nonexecutive-level program staff who had some responsibility for community-related activities, such as institutional consultation, community education, advocacy, and the like. External authorities were "experts" on the research staff of the Community Intervention Project (CIP) who were brought into the agency situation from the university. Three CIP core staff members fulfilled this role. External peers were practitioners who served with the project as field implementers during field research in an earlier phase of the project. They were regularly employed as professionals in social agencies and were introduced as fellow professionals who had implemented the guidelines in the handbook and were present to share their experience with colleagues. Three practitioner-implementers were engaged to conduct these workshops. (For a detailed discussion of training procedures used to ensure a uniform workshop format, see Chapter 8.)

Within the agency, handbooks were circulated to the intended participants previous to the workshop. This was done either by the diffusion agent directly or by a staff member working on his or her behalf. Follow-up questionnaires were provided in the same way. The structure of the overall design of the high-intensity study is depicted in Figure 7.1. Training by the workshop leaders emphasized differentially only the experimental variables concerning locus and status.

The marketing study, then, focused on four different types of diffusion agents relative to agency status and locus. These agents marketed a set of professional innovations contained in a

		Diffusion Agent Organizational Locus	
		Internal	External
Status of Diffusion Agent	Authority	executive agency executive-level staff	expert expert from university research project
	Peer	agency associate	outside agency colleague
		agency program staff	external peer with implementation experience

Figure 7.1:   Diffusion Agent Locus Relative to Target Agency

practitioners' handbook. They employed a standardized work-shop format as the main means of contact, communication, and promotion.

Participating Agencies and Practitioners

Participating agencies and practitioners for the study were selected from among community mental health centers and family service agencies in eight metropolitan communities in the midwestern and northeastern seaboard geographical areas of the United States. We attempted to arrive at as widespread a geographical distribution as possible while keeping costs within financial feasibility. These locations were chosen in part through consultation with the national and regional staffs of the two service delivery systems, based on the availability of a reasonable number of potentially cooperative and stable agency situations. In each of these cities all agency units were included in the sample except those indicated by regional staff to be in an inappropriate condition for conducting a workshop (only starting up and with a skeleton staff, in an intense state of conflict, in the process of relocating, or the like). Remaining agencies were assigned on a random basis to receive one of the four diffusion treatments.

To determine the effects of the alternative diffusion agents (internal/external; authority/peer), a follow-up evaluation was conducted three months after the focal workshop event. Our previous experience with the handbook during the development phase had demonstrated that implementation goals should be "proximate," or short term, attainable within an eight- to twelve-week period. The instrument for gauging utilization of the innovation was the Depth of Utilization Scale (DUS), which specified the degree to which the respondent carried the guideline into action. Hypothetically at least, several things might have occurred during that three-month period: The target users might have simply discarded the handbook; they might have scanned it quickly; they might have studied it carefully; or they might have used it in some systematic way, from minimal involvement with it to full utilization that included a highly successful outcome. The DUS permitted an assessment of such in-depth utilization for each respondent. This DUS is the dependent variable that will be used to determine to what extent diffusion was affected by the diffusion agent treatment received by the respondent. It was the same dependent variable measuring instrument employed in the mass communications substudy.

In addition, directly following the workshop event, each participant filled out a "reactionnaire," which elicited immediate feelings about and attitudes toward the workshop experience. We intended to look at associations, consistent or inconsistent, between these short-run affective reactions and more long-term implemental behavior.

In a secondary analysis, DUS was related to a range of other variables that were obtained through the main questionnaire and in supplementary ways; for example, personal characteristics of the participants and structural features of their organizational situation. A number of attitudinal responses by participants were also examined. The overall design concept may be conveyed through a "journalist" procedural chart (Figure 7.2).

The Sample

We sought to obtain an equal sample of 10 mental health agencies for each of the 4 diffusion agent treatments—40 in all. (The limitation of 40 was determined primarily on the basis of available research funding.)

An additional criterion was city size. Previous research has indicated that there is a differential receptivity to innovation based on urban-rural distinctions and upon the size of the organization toward which the innovation is directed (Rothman, 1974, pp. 516-524). We decided to sample large cities as a means of keeping this variable constant. We assumed that there would be a correlation between city size and agency size, with larger agencies concentrated in the larger cities. The 1970 census data were used to develop a list of the largest metropolitan centers within the target geographical region.

We next compiled a list of NIMH- (federally) funded mental health centers and family service agencies (formally affiliated with the Family Service Association of America) for the designated markets. The federal funding criterion was added to impose additional controls. Such units must be evaluated by NIMH and assessed as conducting acceptable, comprehensive mental health programs. This implies common minimum standards of operation. It also implies a program that is relatively broad and not confined to provision of intrapsychic clinical services. In much more limited, specialized settings, the community and organizational interventions being marketed would not be of any substantial relevance. In addition, these agencies have a common tie to the national NIMH organization. This afforded the possibility of access to centrally collected comparative data on their structures and programs.

The Project Entails the *Diffusion* or *Marketing*

of What	*to Whom*	*by Whom*	*How*	*With What Effect*	*Measurement*
a practitioner's handbook presenting two community-oriented practice innovations, based on social science research generalizations, converted into action guidelines, operationalized, and field tested in applied settings	mental health professionals in community mental health centers and family service agencies in eight large cities in the Midwest and Northwest	four different types of diffusion agents distinguished by locus and status: Agency Executive and Agency Peer (Internal Agents); research project staff member based in the university (External Agents), these four constituting the *Independent Variable*	primarily through use of a standardized workshop within the target agency setting	use of handbook and implementation of innovative strategies by practitioners in their practice situation	Depth of Utilization Scale, constituting the *dependent variable*

Figure 7.2: Journalist Procedural Model

For family service agencies similar factors were taken into account. Affiliation as a member agency of the Family Service Association of America (FSAA) implies a core of common standards and operating procedures. Here again, the national organization is able to serve as a source of formal data and personal information concerning features of the affiliated units.

An initial list of agencies for the sample cities was drawn up using the 1973 *Federally Funded Community Mental Health Centers,* published by NIMH, and the 1974 *Directory of Member Agencies,* published by FSAA. We then consulted with national and regional staff of both agency systems.

On the basis of these consultations, a list of 71 agencies was drawn up within the following metropolitan areas: Boston, New York, Philadelphia, Pittsburgh, Detroit, Chicago, Minneapolis, and Kansas City. While 10 agencies for each treatment was the level intended, we recognized that some of the selected units would refuse to take part. We decided, therefore, to choose a sample of 13 for each treatment, allowing for a reasonable amount of attrition. Should that attrition be higher than we expected, our procedures allowed us to sample further from the overall agency pool we developed initially.

Within each urban area there were considerably more community mental health centers than family service agencies, typically two to three times as many. We gave attention to this in the sampling. We assumed that the sample could include a larger proportion of community mental health centers on the grounds that this is representative of the universe of the settings and agencies being studied.

Some of the agencies had district subunits. We decided to sample only on the basis of central office or headquarters of the agency, regardless of the number of constituent decentralized subunits.

FSAA had in its membership a mixture of nonsectarian and sectarian affiliates (Roman Catholic and Jewish family service agencies). We decided to include all member agencies of FSAA, regardless of sectarian identification. FSAA affiliation implies acceptance of a basic set of norms, standards, and operating procedures that apply to all member units. Such affiliation also implies exposure to common communications and policies emanating from FSAA in New York.

A computer-assisted random sampling procedure was employed for assigning the 13 agencies to each of the 4 treatments. Provision was made for a random initial sample and for systematic replacements from the remainder of the 71 potential agencies within the target cities. This involved the use of a matrix sampling approach (8 cities by 4 workshop leadership treatments by 72 agencies).

Subsequently, the matrix had to be "balanced," based on the given number of agencies available for selection across the four diffusion agent methods. In some cases, not only were there not enough agencies for the sample "pool," but a "balance" between diffusion methods had to be achieved.

After selection of the predetermined number of agencies to diffusion leadership method, an additional pool of agencies was the residual for future use. The procedures we employed followed closely the formulation of Cochran (1963).

We need to add a note of caution regarding the "purity" of this sample selection procedure. Certain assumptions and decisions had to be made that in some cases were arbitrary. Given the fluid nature of field evaluation research, however, this is not unusual. Because of refusals or various difficulties regarding agreement to participate, 14 agencies from the replacement pool were eventually added to the sample.

The process of contacting agencies and obtaining their agreement to participate in workshop programs was difficult and very time consuming. As a consequence, only 37 agencies out of the hoped-for 40 took part in the field study, with some variation in the number for each treatment. One of these failed to forward follow-up data and was not included in the final analysis. In addition, carrying out the diffusion process within various agencies produced situational variations.

As noted above, the DUS was employed to measure utilization of the innovative techniques conveyed in the handbook. A community mental health evaluation program was conducted by Gertz (1974), drawing from the work of Donald L. Kirk-patrick, in which he related outcomes of practitioner training to four types of variables:

(1) *Reactions:* These include trainees' affective reactions to, and opinions on, the content and format of the training experience. This category would also include trainees' plans and desires for future applications of their learning.

(2) *Learnings:* These include facts, concepts, intellectual and motor skills, and affect-laden attitudes.

(3) *On-the-Job Behaviors:* These include changes in the trainees' activities in their task setting from before to after training.

(4) *Results:* These include the effects of posttraining changes in the trainees' behavior (or of changes in others' reactions to the trainees). Such effects could include activities and feelings of coworkers, formal or informal aspects of organizational structure, interorganizational relations, and, ultimately, the welfare of clients served by the trainees and their organizations.

Typically, evaluations of training and assessments of adoption of innovations have tended to focus on those cognitive aspects represented by variables 1 and 2 above. In the high-intensity marketing study, we also examined elements of attitude and cognition. Our major emphasis, however, was on the behavioral criteria suggested by variables 3 and 4 above. We took the view that what was done behaviorally by practitioners, and the consequences brought about by their actions, constituted the strongest indicators of utilization.

A variety of other independent variables from the questionnaire were also available and were used for determining which practitioners had made the greatest use of the handbook. These included personal and demographic characteristics of respondents, their attitudes toward the workshop, their attitudes toward the handbook, and agency factors that might have facilitated or inhibited implementing a guideline.

Two other types of data were also analyzed. The first of these was based on interviews with national and regional mental health professionals regarding the administrative style and atti-

tudes of the directors of the sample agencies (centralized/
decentralized decision making, community relatedness, responsiveness to ideas from the outside; see Appendix F). The second
type was structural data on agencies, made available to us by
the national statistical departments of NIMH and FSAA. These
included such factors as amount of expenditures, size and
composition of the staff, ratio of staff to population served, and
so forth (see Table 9.5, Chapter 9, for the complete list).

Much of the data gathering process was relatively straightforward. Some aspects of that process, however, merit discussion.

Diffusion Agent Influence
and the Naturalistic Field Setting

Because of the naturalistic field setting and the distances
from the CIP research office to the many sample agencies, we
had to rely on agency personnel to assist in various functions.
While agency contact people and coordinators performed their
voluntary tasks generally in a responsible, even admirable, way,
we did not have total standardization of the situation. This
resulted in some local variations in aspects of the work. The
contact person, for example, provided a list of individuals who
would be attending the workshop and who were provided
handbooks beforehand as part of the diffusion plan. Some of
the individuals listed to attend the workshop did not appear,
while others not listed were recorded as having attended. Some
degree of shuffling around had taken place in the course of the
normal ups and downs of agency life.

We were faced with making choices about how to proceed
with the analysis. One approach would have been to include in
the analysis only those staff who had attended a workshop. This
was considered and rejected on the grounds that it excluded
others who had received a handbook and were part of the
diffusion agents' target market, even though they did not
appear at the workshop. Because of our interest in the total
impact of the diffusion agent, including workshop aspects, we
chose to include as subjects to receive a follow-up questionnaire
all agency staff members whose names appeared on diffusion

documents and were thus included in the diffusion agents' overall web of influence. The study focus, it should be remembered, was not on workshop diffusion per se, but on diffusion agents of various types using a high-intensity mode of contact and communication. Our results, therefore, may be conceptualized as embracing all staff members in the agency who became implicated in the activities of a given type of diffusion agent (according to locus/status criteria) by having participated in a workshop or having been targeted to receive a handbook, or both. We made the reasonable assumption that diffusion agent influence included periods both preceding and following the workshop: before, when the workshop was arranged for, announced, and handbooks distributed, and afterward, when practice innovations were being carried out by the staff and arrangements were made for completion and pickup of the follow-up questionnaire. Generally, we will refer to this as the "workshop approach," while recognizing that the treatment expands beyond the workshop as such.

To be sure, the workshop was the main thrust of the diffusion agent's activity. Approximately 90 percent of the questionnaire respondents indicated that they had attended a workshop. This means, however, that another 10 percent experienced the diffusion agent's efforts or presence in another way—in particular, receiving the handbook directly from the agent and becoming involved in the follow-up activities conducted by, or in the name of, the agent.

This approach contains the disadvantage of having some areas of uncertainty in terms of specific exposures and involvements of respondents in the diffusion agent's effort. It possesses the counterbalancing advantage of greater completeness with regard to the diffusion agent's scope of impact than would the alternative of including only those who participated in the workshop experience. Our evaluation was designed to determine what occurred to all individuals recorded as related to the diffusion effort (those listed to receive a handbook or those who filled out at the workshop a registration form or reactionnaire): Did they read the handbook, study it, use it systematically or unsystematically, and so on?

As a general review, there were 37 agencies that participated by distributing handbooks and having a workshop. Of these, 9 were family service agencies; 28 were community mental health centers. (One of the family service agencies had to be dropped from later analyses because follow-up evaluation forms were not received.) There were 711 individuals recorded as part of the diffusion agents' effort: individuals who received handbooks and/or attended a workshop. Among the subjects, 374 returned a follow-up questionnaire (a 52.6 percent return rate). Among these respondents, 336 (89.9 percent) indicated that they had attended a workshop. In examining the return rate, we must keep in mind that 99 individuals among the subjects, about one-seventh, left the agency by the time of the follow-up. A tabulation that provides specific descriptive details concerning the nature of the sample may be found in Appendix E.

Sampling and engagement of the sample in the diffusion process was difficult and time consuming. Some of the problems of naturalistic field studies, where controls are more difficult to maintain, are revealed. Chapter 8 will describe field issues and problems. The findings will need to be assessed in the light of these difficulties and limitations.

Data Analysis Procedures

After completing the initial analysis with contingency tables and its associated statistics (as described in Chapter 4), two other analysis strategies were used. First, a combination of the AID3 (Automatic Interaction Detector) and MCA (Multiple Classification Analysis) were used (Andrews, 1973). These were developed by the University of Michigan's Institute for Social Research. They are multivariate analysis techniques for nominal-ordinal social science data. These techniques permit an examination of the relationship among significant independent variables. Second, after transforming the nominal and ordinal variables using Lingoes (1973) techniques, a discriminant analysis of all predictors in relation to DU was completed. This technique permits the selection of those important variables that can discriminate between different levels of utilization.

We felt that a combination of these three analysis techniques would be most useful with the data available for an examination of utilization. In effect, not only would the range of variables significantly associated with utilization be identified, but it would also be possible to discern the relationship among these significant variables, including their relative weighting or strength with regard to association with utilization.

Before going on to report the findings of the study, we will discuss the field program and its problems. We were concerned with discovering the dynamics of the social marketing process in personal contact diffusion. A qualitative description and analysis, rather than a quantitative display, is necessary for this purpose.

References

Andrews, F. *Multiple classification analysis.* Ann Arbor: Institute for Social Research, University of Michigan, 1973.

Cochran, W. G. *Sampling techniques* (2nd ed.). New York: John Wiley, 1963.

Coleman, J. S., Katz, E. & Menzel, H. *Medical innovation: A diffusion study.* Indianapolis: Bobbs-Merril, 1966.

Gertz, B. *Continuing education in mental health: Training models in rural mental health.* Mimeograph, Fort Logan Mental Health Center, Denver, July 1974.

Gross, N., Giaquinta, J. B., & Bernstein, M. *Implementing organizational innovation.* New York: Basic Books, 1971.

Lingoes, J. C. The Guttman-Lingoes. In *Non Metric Program Series.* Ann Arbor, MI: Mathesis, 1973.

Rothman, J. *Planning and organizing for social change: Action guidelines from social science research.* New York: Columbia University Press, 1974.

Senders, V. *Measurement and statistics.* New York: Oxford University Press, 1958.

University of Michigan Statistical Research Laboratory. *MIDAS manual.* Ann Arbor: Author, 1975.

CHAPTER 8

SOME FIELD PROBLEMS IN INTERPERSONAL SOCIAL MARKETING

A Brief Look Forward

In this chapter we are concerned with the realities of field research and some of the problems and insights such realities bring. We discuss the processes by which we secured cooperation and participation of our target agencies and examine a few of the reasons some agencies chose not to participate. We review briefly both the preparation and follow-up procedures for the workshops, and examine various modes of influencing agency directors and relate these to patterns of executive decision making in agencies. We conclude with a retrospective of procedural problems we encountered in our field research and add a note about field response and staff morale.

These field aspects of the study will be of particular interest to some readers and provide context for the findings. Those primarily interested in the findings may wish to move on directly to the next chapter.

Preparatory Work

The design of the study implies an orderly and logical series of steps and activities. This leaves much unsaid. A great deal of thought and effort had to go toward making contacts with agencies, explaining the purpose of the study, gaining cooperation, distributing handbooks, arranging and conducting workshops, monitoring the process, obtaining evaluative feedback, responding to unforeseen circumstances, and so on. In addition to gathering data, this was an action-research field experiment in which the field research staff functioned as change agents or social marketers in promoting innovative practices. The agencies we were attempting to affect were busy places, swayed and bombarded by multiple pressures. Harried agency directors and burdened staff members experienced our attempt to instigate innovative practices on their part as only one of myriad other competing attempts.

Much preparatory work went into creating the right climate for access to community mental health and family service agencies. Too often, researchers doing field studies neglect interactional facets of the work. We had here a complex task in organizational influence on marketing in addition to more conventional technical activities.

Contacts with National
and Regional Staffs

We began by securing the support of a key contact person at both the NIMH and FSAA national offices. We gave these two individuals full information on the purposes and methods of our study, and we sought their advice.

FSAA reviewed with us our target markets and agency sample. They alerted us to possible trouble spots and assisted us with strategy suggestions for coping with these potential problems. They also provided us with upper-echelon entree to their regional staff.

NIMH is a much larger system. Its structure is not as stable or controlled as that of the FSAA. With NIMH it was necessary to go to regional office staff for the same kind of information that was provided at the national level in FSAA. The NIMH regional officials were uniformly receptive and provided much useful knowledge. Though formal approval was not necessary in gaining access to the agencies, they served as a source of legitimation in our initial contacts with the agencies.

As we proceeded, national and regional staff people were kept well informed of our progress. As actual field operations began, each regional representative was sent an individual letter, a handbook, and a list of agencies from their regions that were to be included in our sample.

While the understanding and cooperation of regional people were solicited, care was taken to see that such support did not become intrusive. Several regional representatives inquired concerning responses they should give to agencies asking their opinion about participating in the study. To each request we sent a standard written response:

> We are, of course, eager to gain the participation of local units, and if you are of the belief that such voluntary involvement is justified and appropriate, we trust you will convey your opinion to those making inquiries. What we would like to avoid is a sense of pressure to participate that a local director may come to feel, and, thus, pass on to staff of his agency. In that case, the extent of utilization of the handbook might be related to pressure placed on staff by the executive, rather than the particular type of workshop that is conducted in the agency as a method of diffusion. This is a subtle point, as are so many others in the profession; but I hope this brief explanation of the issue as we see it will place you in a position to respond comfortably to any advice asked of you by affiliates.

Follow-up correspondence kept the regional representative abreast of developments throughout the marketing study.

Contacts with Agencies

We formulated an assertive outreach procedure for gaining access to agencies in the sample. It consisted of several steps. First, a letter was sent to the agency director describing the project, proving a copy of the handbook, and indicating the desire to arrange a workshop. Our previous national and regional consultations convinced us that a formal approach to the director was the most advisable means of beginning the process of arranging for a workshop in agencies. In our initial letter the cooperation of specified regional and national staff was clearly indicated. For the indigenous or internal workshop leader approaches, the director was invited to select an appropriate staff member (executive staff or program staff) to attend the workshop in Ann Arbor. For the external leadership approaches, the director was asked to allow a member of our research staff to conduct a workshop within the agency. In terms of phasing the work, the internal leadership letters were sent first because this required a longer process: a university conference followed by a workshop later within the agency, led by the individual who had attended the campus-based conference. The letter contained appropriate information concerning the time of the conference, how costs would be met by the research project, and so on. The director was also informed that a member of the CIP staff would telephone within a week to discuss the matter further, answer any questions, and make arrangements for further steps.

The external leadership (CIP staff-administered) letters gave additional information about the time periods during which the workshop could take place, number of hours to be allowed for the workshop, optimal number of staff to attend (15 to 20), and how they should be chosen (voluntary participation). It also pointed out that the handbooks were free and the workshop would be conducted at no cost to the agency.

Next, within a week we made direct follow-up telephone calls to the agency director. These calls were by CIP's director and assistant director because we thought it important that approximately equal status contact be made. Reaching the agency directors was a time-consuming, convoluted, tedious, and frustrating process. Agency directors are individuals with many and varied responsibilities. A great many of these take place at other than their desks—in the community, for example, at meetings, within other private and governmental agencies, and so forth. It quickly became obvious that directors play a highly nonuniform role in a turbulent organizational environment. This presented a considerable number of problems and obstacles as far as the objectives of our study were concerned.

After contact was eventually made with the director (or in some instances with a designated substitute), a standard telephone interview was conducted to clarify the original letter and to arrange next steps. This interview amplified on the information contained in the letter and made it clear to the agency what its responsibilities would be in connection with our efforts.

Our third step in cementing the sample structure occurred when the agency agreed to participate in the study. At this point we requested that they designate (for the internal treatment) an individual to attend the university conference. For the external treatment we asked them to appoint a liaison contact person within the agency who would take responsibility for arrangements concerning the workshop to be conducted by a CIP staff member. Information and materials were then mailed immediately to these individuals, with a copy and a memorandum to the agency director. This was a part of our ongoing effort to make sure that the director was fully informed and his commitments reinforced. The understanding was that the program was being carried out as an activity approved by the agency director through an appointed agent to expedite its implementation.

If an agency refused to participate for one reason or another, the CIP assistant director, who was coordinating sampling procedures, was notified immediately. Using a standard random procedure, he selected a replacement from the agency pool. A total of 13 replacements were required. This caused the administrative workings of our field operations to become quite complex.

We employed many techniques for managing and monitoring the contact process. Desk charts were maintained for individuals making calls. These included such information as by whom and when the initial call was made to each agency, the results of the call, and any additional notes. Wall charts indicating the status of each sample agency were prominently displayed. Schedules of field staff to visit agencies in the external treatments were kept current at all times. A guide for the initial telephone call was prepared and distributed to the callers to ensure that all agencies received adequate and consistent information. We structured our operations with a clear division of responsibilities to assure consistent follow-up in making and receiving calls. We adapted our office hours to differing time zones. We held ongoing training sessions with office staff to ensure that such matters as calls to the project were handled courteously and professionally. Rapid communication was constantly stressed and adhered to in scheduling workshops and replacing agencies.

To influence agency decision to participate, our staff stressed certain factors in telephone discussions. These included legitimation from regional offices and presentation of the project in part as a service to the agency and the field. We also pointed out the specific benefits that could accrue to the agency and/or its staff. A valued benefit in internal treatments was an expense-free conference at the Ann Arbor campus of the University of Michigan. Benefits for external treatments included the fact that the workshop might be conducted as a staff meeting and as part of the agency staff development program, consultation service, and free supportive materials (the handbook). We also pointed out that research evidence would be gathered that could help mental health and family service agencies do a better job in disseminating new practice techniques. Finally, we alerted the agencies to the opportunities for increased funding of the agency through expansion of community-related programs in accordance with emerging federal legislation and guidelines. Responses in terms of sequencing and timing were kept tight and exact ("I will call you back within two days," for example).

Agency Refusals

About a dozen agencies refused to take part in the study. They expressed a variety of reasons for declining the workshop experience. Principal among these were:

(1) Time constraints—the organization could not fit the workshop into its schedule:

> In view of the current pressures, I really do not see how we can justify the use of time and the kind of planning required for setting up the staff workshop as proposed. It might appear to be

nothing more than setting another meeting, but it would have other implications for us now, and I think the timing makes it impossible.

(2) External environmental factors inhibited participation (an intern strike in New York City, for example):

The press of business here and the closeness of the meeting to the Passover holidays makes our attendance impossible.

(3) The agency felt that it already had an active training program or satisfactory professional situation and did not need outside assistance:

We have a well-established plan of staff education and development, and our specific plans have been set up for the year.

(4) The executive did not have time to study and act on the matter:

I regret the tardiness of our response to you in regard to your project and proposal to offer a training session here. Firstly, this tardiness might suggest disorganization, but I prefer to believe it reflects how hyper-busy we've been over the last months; so much so that I could write a book on all the things we're behind on, except I haven't got time.

(5) The agency could not do it at this time because of other priorities:

Our Director of Counseling feels we are long overdue on a client attitude study and prefers to invest any new time that may present itself to that area.

(6) The agency would only participate jointly with other local agencies; it was not willing to follow the one agency, one treatment arrangement.

(7) The agency felt it was not ready or sufficiently well organized for the program. Staff was "not together."

(8) The agency was not doing enough community-related work, having a mainly clinical focus.

The diffusion literature is replete with findings about organizations declining to consider adoption of innovative ideas and practices. The extent of refusals is, therefore, not unexpected or unusual. It is obvious that in a study such as this, there will be a turndown phenomenon based on overt reasons, such as those we've cited. Turndown needs to be anticipated and planned for, however, and actions of various sorts taken to keep it within bounds.

Campus Conference for
Internal Treatments

Two separate conferences were held for the internal workshop leaders, one for executive staff members and one for program or peer staff. These took place one week apart. A letter was sent to each participant, preparing him or her for taking part, stating expectations, and indicating detail work required.

A similar memorandum was sent to the agency director. Its purpose was to gain the director's backing in having the agency representative attend the conference, conduct a subsequent workshop within the agency, and arrange for follow-up evaluation within the agency.

A standard workshop format was used during the morning session. In the afternoon session participants were trained in the use of the same workshop format and prepared for subsequent stages. This was also the workshop format used in the external treatment when CIP staff conducted workshops within the agency itself.

The two university workshops were somewhat different in their development. Executives were more difficult to bring together than peers. Peers found it more difficult to follow through with their own agency workshops. Executives were more interested in the guideline on establishing new programs and services than were the peers and wanted more time spent on it. Peers were more interested in the guideline on fostering participation and were more attuned to the practical use of the handbook in their own agency situation.

Immediately after the participants returned to their agencies following the workshop, a letter was sent to each of them requesting a date for the workshop they would be conducting and a list of names and addresses of agency personnel expected to participate. We told them of our interest in general reactions and comments they might have about their workshops, and we reminded them of our intention to perform a three-month follow-up.

When we received the names and dates of the workshops (by phone and letter), we sent packages of materials to each of the university workshop participants. They, in turn, were to distribute these to participants within their agencies.

We had various impressions concerning differences in conducting a central workshop for internal executives and for internal peers. It was much more difficult to get executives than peers to a central conference. Executives are, apparently, very much tied up in their agency situations. Only 8 out of an intended 13 participants were obtained in the executive treatment (including 1 who was trained at a makeup meeting); 12 peers were obtained with much less difficulty. Even at the makeup session, 2 of 3 executives who agreed to participate did not appear after all because of emergency situations or generally unpredictable schedules.

This was the reverse of our anticipation. We thought at the outset that it would be administratively easier for the agency executive to arrange for a delegate to attend a conference from among his or her small, immediate, administrative staff (that included him or her), rather than to decide on and seek out a person from the much broader range of program staff.

Once at the conference, however, it seemed easier and quicker for executives to arrange follow-up workshops in their agencies. Workshop date confirmations came in much quicker and included the entire group who attended the on-campus conference. The executives, apparently, have the authority and control to move decisively in this direction. Two of the peers were unable to schedule workshops in their agencies and, subsequently, had to be dropped from the sample. The others were slower than the executives in scheduling the workshops and returning registration and questionnaire materials. Seven of the peers were sent at least one letter reminding them to return the materials. Some others required a series of both written and telephone communications.

As feedback from the agency workshops was received, it began to appear that in the internal, compared to the external, workshops (particularly the peer), things were done more sloppily. Some of the peers, for example, were lax in distributing handbooks before the workshop and were not as diligent as they should have been in recording who had received handbooks in their agencies.

Procedure for External Treatments

External workshop treatments made it necessary for us to schedule a training session within each agency. That session was conducted by a member of our Community Intervention Project staff. Chronologically, we set this series of appointments following the two campus-based conferences. A detailed and complex set of steps and interactions ensued.

After the initial mailing of letters and handbooks to the agency directors in our two subsamples (external experts and external peers), we spent approximately two months negotiating with the agencies for dates, times, and places of workshops. Virtually all of this was done by phone. A contact person in each agency was designated to make workshop preparations, distribute handbooks in advance, and assist in data gathering. With a date set, we sent a form letter to the agency contact person, confirming the workshop date and requesting a list of names and agency mailing addresses of participants in the workshop.

The workshop packet resembled that sent to our university conference participants. It included a cover letter to our contact person giving the name of our CIP staff member who would be conducting the workshop, explaining what was in the packet, and indicating how the materials should be distributed. A form letter for each participant was enclosed in each handbook, giving the date, time, and place of the workshop and the names of the workshop leader and the agency contact person.

In follow-up communications, we suggested that the contact person arrange a meeting with the workshop leader during the hour previous to the event. This gave them an opportunity to share information and complete final preparations.

Six members (or former members) of our CIP staff conducted workshops. To assure consistency, we developed uniform procedures.[1] These were used at each of the two university training conferences, and each of our workshop fieldworkers attended at least one of the conferences in order to observe the procedures and obtain clarification (see Appendix G for the workshop format).

We should note that a substantive portion of the workshop time was given over to pairs of participants using the handbook and various log forms we developed to work on actual agency problems. These were later shared and critiqued in a total group session.

Following the university conferences, we held a training session for the external peer workshop leaders, all of whom, by virtue of their association with CIP, were familiar with our objectives and methods. In addition to focusing on the conduct of the workshop, the training session covered a number of other responsibilities of external peer workshop leaders. The CIP project core staff took responsibility for recruiting participating agencies, scheduling the workshops, forwarding handbooks and other background information to agency contacts and workshop participants, and the general housekeeping matters that accompany any research endeavor.

We standardized a reporting schedule for the workshop leaders in a form that paralleled exactly the components of the workshop agenda. It provided a check for the leader and for the research staff as to whether all components had been covered. In monitoring this process, a project staff member attended four workshop sessions as an observer and recorded the events on the same forms used by the workshop leaders. This constituted a cross-validation procedure. On all factors considered critical for the research design, the reports of the workshop leader and the observer were identical. This gave some measure of assurance that procedures were consistent. In addition, later findings indicated no significant differences in participant responses among the individual workshop leaders, although there were such differences for workshop leaders aggregated into treatments. This also suggests fairly uniform workshop delivery.

Several monitoring techniques were used to ensure that each training situation was implemented properly. As the workshop leader reports were returned, they were reviewed by CIP staff for completeness and possible problems. One follow-up call was made to the agency contact person after the workshops to discuss the workshop experience. Any problems or misunderstandings were dealt with at that time. This follow-up further set the stage for contact-person assistance in the evaluation that would follow.

Additionally, we used the crosscheck between observers and external workshop leaders mentioned earlier as a monitoring technique. We did not feel it was necessary to have similar monitoring tools for workshops conducted by internal workshop leaders. For these, the project-initiated input consisted of the two standardized university conferences. We assumed that indigenous leaders would use variations in their own presentations, although they received identical training in the basic format. For external workshops the project-initiated input to the innovation process was the workshop at each individual agency, and that had to be standardized.

Postworkshop Procedures

Much follow-up was necessary after the workshop presentations. External workshop leaders, for example, serving as field staff, had to file registration forms on their return, providing basic personal information about each individual who attended or who was given a handbook in connection with the workshop. They also brought completed reactionnaires (short questionnaires) indicating participant response to the workshop experience. Internal peers lagged behind executives in returning materials.

Telephone interviews with the internal workshop leaders followed receipt of registration forms and reactionnaires, soliciting subjective information on a variety of matters pertaining to the workshop. These included how the workshop went, reactions of participants to the handbook and workshop format, positive or negative factors that might influence participants in future use of the handbook, the extent to which the agenda was followed, and the general composition of the workshop group. The internal workshop leaders were also asked about discrepancies between the original proposed list of attendees and those on the registration list. Information concerning any follow-up activities the agency itself might be contemplating was solicited. The workshop took place in the spring, and workshop leaders were all reminded of our proposed fall follow-up evaluation. We sought their aid in serving as in-agency coordinators for this follow-up. All agreed to assist us in this way.

For external workshops, CIP staff conducted similar telephone interviews with agency contact persons. Again, all expressed a willingness to participate in follow-up activities.

As the time for the follow-up approached, the agency coordinator was sent a packet of questionnaires, each individually enclosed in a stamped, self-addressed envelope, and a list of persons to whom the questionnaires should be distributed. In addition, standardized instructions for collecting and returning the questionnaires were included. A phone contact a week later confirmed that the material had been received and distributed. The involvement of an agency-based coordinator led to a high rate of return for this type of decentralized evaluation.

Field Operations: A Retrospective

AN INFLUENCE PROCESS

Our field operations constituted a complex and often difficult process that included elements of administration, salesmanship, and data collection, all tightly interwoven. As a social marketing study/diffusion experiment, an influence process was at its core. The staff took care to build an aura of legitimation from the top down. Rewards and benefits of various kinds were offered and reemphasized in a series of different kinds of communications. Personal contact supplemented written communication by phone and in face-to-face relationships. There was a continuing stream of reminders, follow-through contacts, and firm time boundaries for responses and further steps.

We found that it was possible, after penetrating the agency boundary at the director entry point, to establish firm working relationships and gain ample assistance within the organization. The contact person, later designated questionnaire coordinator, typically became identified with the study and served in the role of adjunct project fieldworker within the agency setting. This on-site aid was enormously valuable.

THE AGENCY DIRECTOR AS GATEKEEPER

A factor materially influencing the conduct of the study was the critical nature of the position of director within the systems we were attempting to affect. The director was the all-important gatekeeper, controlling the pathways into the organizations of our sample. We had been strongly advised by the national and regional contacts to seek access by way of the director in order to gain authorization for a workshop. Experience in the study verified that this was probably the quickest, most expeditious, and in some cases the only possible way of instituting a workshop, especially in working with widely scattered agencies in a large geographic region. Nevertheless, this mode of entry presented obstacles and frustrations of large order.

In general, agency executives in these systems are centrifugal individuals with role overload. They seem to be inundated by volumes of mail and multiple tasks and responsibilities. A great deal of intensive follow-up by telephone was required to gain their attention in the face of all kinds of competing claims and demands. Many phone calls were required, first to get through to the executive, then to cue him or her to the project and the handbook. (Many couldn't remember receiving it, hadn't gotten to it yet, discarded it, passed it on to someone else, put it aside for later reading in a high pile of marginal material, and so forth.) Many executives could not locate the communication or insisted that it had not arrived. Numerous times we sent follow-up packets; in some instances, we sent 2 follow-up mailings. Of the 65 or so letters that went out, only 2 directors took up our invitation to initiate a collect call to us. In some cases the director's secretary was the key contact person, implementing the process for, and in place of, the director.

After making operational contact with the executive, the next step was following the process through to the point where the matter was assigned to an appropriate staff member. When this was accomplished, such a program person expedited the process quickly.

The quality of the experience in working through agency directors is reflected in an example drawn from our field notes. The notations below concern contacts over a one-month period with a large mental health center in New England:

4/4   Dr. C was not available.

4/7   Dr. C was at a meeting.

4/8   I reached Dr. C. He couldn't locate our mailed packet. Thinks some staff person had picked it up. Will try to find out who has it and call back.

4/15   I have not heard from Dr. C. I called. There was no answer at the center.

4/16   Got through. Dr. C is out of town till Tuesday. Spoke to his secretary. They have not been able to trace the packet as yet—still looking. I said I would airmail out a duplicate.

4/28   I called. Dr. C said they are interested. The name of Mr. T was given as the contact person.

4/29   I called T. Had not read the materials yet. Said he will call back after he does.

This erratic and eccentric experience with directors seems to cast doubt on diffusion methods using mailings and lacking the persistent intensity of personal follow through. Later we will compare the results of low-intensity and high-intensity approaches.

MODES OF INFLUENCING THE DIRECTOR

Because the crucial, initial decision was in the hands of the directors, our approach to them was carefully designed to overcome resistance to the innovation and to stress aspects of the undertaking that would provide benefits in their task environments. The director's position as a bureaucratic functionary led us to rely heavily upon legitimation from higher organizational levels. We devoted much effort to building a basis for this kind of bureaucratic legitimation. We exploited the benefit of winning the approval of, or at least not disturbing, hierarchical superordinates. Equal status contact between executives in the project and the executive of the agency was another way in which we respected the position of the director.

The character of the handbook itself was an important element in gaining directors' attention and winning their interest. The handbook was highly applied in character and written in the idiom of the world of social agencies. It was attractive, colorful, and problem oriented. Indeed, in many frenetic telephone contacts, communication was sometimes achieved when one party or the other referred to the "booklet with the bright blue cover." The handbook was interlaced with agency-based examples, and partially written in the language of practitioners. The latter constituted another form of legitimation, emanating in this instance from professionals in the field. In a sense, the practitioners and agency executives quoted in the handbook were saying, "See how I carried this out; it really works."

The executive of an agency is concerned with the efficiency of his operation and, in particular, with the risk of failure. The legitimation provided by other agency-based professionals, speaking in the handbook, brought across the messages that disseminating this to agency staff would be a worthwhile use of time and that there was not a high risk of damage in using the handbook; it had been checked out by other operational people and found a viable tool in similar agency settings.

In written communication and in telephone contact, however, we took executives' managerial concerns into account. We stated, for example, that more staff involvement in community-related programming could contribute to increased funding for the agency because of new federal programs and guidelines that were giving more attention to this area. We stressed the fact that the handbook was free and would not require use of agency financial resources. We made the same point with regard to the provision of a workshop by the project. We also pointed out that increasing the skill of staff in working with community pressures could take part of this load off the director's shoulders.

We appealed strongly to chances of increased professional and organizational status. The executive's agency had been selected and would be given an opportunity to participate in a research study that was sponsored by a major university and funded by a leading mental health research organization. The executive would be in a position to contribute to research that might be helpful in making professional advances in the field. Prestige was connected with such involvements.

We pointed up certain practice-related advantages, as well. For example, two benefits of using the handbook guidelines were improved services to populations of clients and better community relations. We gave less emphasis to these, however, based on the CIP staff's judgment that these would be of less moment in gaining executives' approval.

One might say that executives constantly find themselves in cost-benefit caldrons. We attempted to highlight benefits while placing less emphasis on such costs as taking time away from other vital needs, using up agency resources in the wrong directions, and being disapproved by one's organizational superiors or professional peers. While this aspect of diffusion did not enter into formal data gathering aspects of the research design, the marketing plan relied heavily upon benefit-conveying persuasion.

The nature of the innovation being disseminated may account for the degree of success achieved in entering the organization with an innovation, compared to other attempts such as, for example, Glaser and Ross (1971). In that study, the innovation required a total organizational decision to implement, including a decision to allocate substantial agency resources to this activity and to change various routines and assignments within the organization. In our study the innovative methods being diffused could be carried out at the level of the individual professional within the organization and in the context of his or her ordinary assignments. Each practitioner would make a personal decision about integrating the innovative technique into his or her practice. At the level of the director, he or she needed to make a decision as to whether the project should be given access to these individual practitioners through the medium of a workshop experience.

PATTERNS OF DIRECTOR DECISION MAKING

In the course of negotiations with directors for acceptance of a workshop, we encountered four different decision-making patterns among them:

A Decision and Response Made Directly by the Director

A number of directors communicated acceptance of the workshop for their agencies during the course of the first contact or in a subsequent contact. The directors conveyed personal responsibility and authority for the decision. Only in a few instances, however, was this done as a "solo" performance. Ordinarily, some other staff member in the agency was consulted or informed previous to the announcement of approval by the director. In this pattern, and in the others, it was discernible that few directors function as full-fledged patriarchs or tyrants in the agency setting. Mental health agencies have been described as possessing a "human relations" organizational climate, meaning that decision making is to some degree shared. Even when the director made and transmitted the decision himself or herself, there was evidence in most instances that communication with others had taken place in the process.

Decision Referred to Another
Administrative Actor in the Organization

In some cases the director notified us that the matter of the workshop had been turned over to another individual in the organization. Sometimes this was someone with a general administrative role, such as the assistant director. Sometimes it was someone with a particular programmatic responsibility, such as in-service training, consulting, and education. In most cases, however, the transmittal was made with the explicit or implicit understanding that the director favored a positive decision, at least in principle. In other words, the director had already screened the request and found it acceptable. The ultimate decision, however, was left to an individual with more direct involvement or interest in the particular area. The request had been routed into the organization for active consideration by a relevant decision maker, rather than blocked or deflected.

Decision Referred to a Decentralized
Advisory or Decision-Making Group

In some cases it was clear that the director was not assuming a role of influence in deciding the matter. In these agencies there appeared to be a pattern of decentralized decision making with regard to some range of issues, among which the workshop matter was included. The director was serving here as a transmittal agent, most often not taking an active screening role (although if the request had appeared extremely noxious to him or her, he or she might have deflected it).

Many times the term "advisory committee" was used in notifying us of the disposition of the matter. Such committees sometimes appeared to be rather general. Others appeared to deal more narrowly with matters such as training programs. Our experience was that this pattern often delays or precludes an adoption decision, and we noted several apparently contributing factors. Participation in the decision by different staff may generate conflict based on interunit competition. Staff members with clinical commitments may feel that prestige and resources allocated to their unit might be threatened by a turn toward community intervention. Staff committees may also perceive a proposed innovation as a negative reflection on current functioning. Some staff may oppose the innovation because they fear a change in their role definition and doubt their own ability to assume new responsibilities. Some may fear that the innovation would result in additional responsibilities. Lack of effective communication in a decentralized decision structure may result in misunderstanding of the innovation or inadequate sharing of information among individuals and committees involved in the decision.

While use of a collective decision-making mechanism seemed to retard or endanger affirmative organizational response in this study, we could hypothesize that, in those instances in which a positive joint decision was made, this paved the way for effective follow through later; that is, because of collective commitment to the program, the greatest degree of subsequent utilization of the innovation would likely ensue. With the data currently available to us, we were not able to trace through this supposition.

Decision Referred to a Functional
Administrative Unit of the Organization

Here the decision is referred to a functional or a program branch of the organization. For community mental health centers this was, in most instances, the Consultation and Education Unit. Under this arrangement, the director was conveying previous general organizational approval and passing the matter on for implementation or for a programmatic decision (the workshop would be consistent with program goals; there was room in the schedule; the staff would be willing to cooperate; and the like). This is slightly different from the second decision-making pattern we discussed above. The quality of the process implied that an operational branch of the organization, rather than a delegated administrator, would decide. Our experience indicates that this pattern frequently results in a decision to adopt. It is not surprising that the Education and Consultation Unit supported the innovation. This is the unit most likely to benefit in terms of increased resources and prestige from more emphasis on community intervention. Also, staff of this unit are most likely to be familiar with community interaction and committed to community intervention. As the unit in closest contact with the general community, it is also most likely to perceive the need for better community involvement and to see the applicability of the guidelines to its situation.

Procedural Problems

A number of procedural problems were encountered that may be peculiar to this type of marketing field research. For example, scheduling created difficulties as the field study was under way. Matching workshop leader schedules to those of the agencies was time consuming and created obstacles to participation. The field study was caught in a squeeze between delayed publication of the handbook and an attempt to avoid the summer months, when many agency activities disband or slow down. The difficulty encountered in implementing the diffusion process in the presence of such time constraints suggests the need for both flexibility and firmness in planning. The task of scheduling agency workshops was large enough to have warranted an additional staff person to handle administrative arrangements.

There were, as we mentioned, delays in publication of materials. The handbook was not ready until two months after the date initially projected. This necessitated the rescheduling of other arrangements, such as the conferences and the carrying out of contacts and workshops on a contracted schedule. Our planning was constantly susceptible to the actions of external organizations and forces.

Another problem was contagion among agencies within cities. We anticipated that each agency in each sample city would constitute a separate unit and treatment. There was more informal communication among agencies and their staffs, however, than we had counted on. People in agencies, for example, spoke with each other about their differing relationships with the project. Some contacted the project for an explanation of the variations. In addition, agencies in some instances wished to join with one another across different treatment modalities in common training sessions. It was necessary to interpret and hold a firm position concerning keeping to individual agency workshops.

Illustratively, we discovered that Temple University was involved in a mental health continuing education project in Philadelphia. This project was also oriented to community outreach skills and was sponsored by the Council on Social Work Education. Some of our conference attendees in both the executive and the peer treatments wanted to do their workshops jointly with other agencies in the community who were also involved in the Temple project. We urged them not to. We also spoke to the dean and project director at Temple, requesting them not to intermix the two programs. They agreed to proceed in compliance with our request.

Field Responses and Staff Morale

Despite the difficulties posed by a fluid, open-ended field setting, our staff was able to schedule 37 workshops in 8 different cities and to achieve a reasonably high return rate for the utilization questionnaires. We note also, with a sense of satisfaction, that reactionnaire responses by workshop participants were markedly favorable (see Table 9.9, Chapter 9, and Table 10.1, Chapter 10). Cordial, professional relationships were established with contact persons and other agency staff in the course of arranging and conducting workshops. Direct favorable feedback from these individuals was a psychological element that contributed to research staff morale and helped sustain the effort.

Two typical letters, reflecting a considerably larger number, illustrate the quality of the feedback regarding both the handbook and the workshop experience:

Members of our staff have found "A Handbook for Community Mental Health and Family Service Professionals" very useful as a planning and organizing tool. We are currently preparing to run a training program in Child Development for interested staff of child-serving agencies in Southeast Philadelphia. In addition, we are also promoting and facilitating the sponsorship of community run play-groups for pre-school children.

In our planning around these two tasks, we have found the section of the handbook on "Fostering Participation" particularly relevant. The exercise offers a rational framework with which to articulate and pursue specific goals, and the concept of "relevant benefits" is providing us with a practical strategy for approaching the community.

* * *

On behalf of the staff of the J. Mental Health/Mental Retardation Center who participated in the Community Intervention Skills work-ship . . . please accept my sincere thanks and appreciation for select-ing us for inclusion in your NIMH study.

I know I speak for the entire group when I say how pleased we were with A.G.'s presentation and ensuing discussion. I also personally feel that the handbook will be useful in my own practice and in teaching assignments with students and staff.

We know you will be contacting us again by letter in the Fall, and I hope we can report success in our attempts to apply the guidelines. I've already begun implementation!

The testimonial letter has something of a checkered history in consumer marketing. We did not, in either of our social marketing studies, examine its use as a source of evaluation. Of course, not all responses were on the favorable side. One internal workshop leader informed us that a staff member, after reading the handbook, decided not to attend the workshop. The handbook was returned to the workshop leader with the following note enclosed:

I've decided not to attend the workshop on Monday so please scratch my name from the list. I have only one question for this guy. How much and why did NIMH pay for a 7 year research project that came up with the original ideas that 1) you should reward desired behavior and 2) to start a new community program, begin with a small group and enlarge it?

There was, of course, a great deal more to both our social marketing efforts and the work of the Community Intervention Project. Such occasional chastisements, however, had the wholesome effect of requiring us to keep our sense of importance in proper perspective. Notwithstanding the incidental efforts to assure an appropriate humility on our part, in-process, informal responses were overwhelmingly positive; and, for researchers with strong applied research interests, this type of real-world confirmation of usefulness was a sustaining force. One wonders what would have become of staff morale in the event that feedback from the field had been uniformly negative and/or disparaging. It appears that in operationalizing this type of demanding and extended field experiment, the question of staff morale is a matter that needs particularly to be taken into account.

Note

1. Principal among these were: (1) to participate in a one-day orientation program (for which we compensated them at the regular university consulting rate); (2) to conduct three to six workshops in participating agencies using a standard workshop format; (3) to record the experience on a standard reporting form; (4) to meet with the agency contact person one hour before the workshop to obtain final clarifications and complete final arrangements; (5) to phone the agency contact person two or three days before the workshop to confirm the appointment and arrangements; and (6) to obtain participant information on registration and reactionnaire forms.

Reference

Glaser, E. M., & Ross, H. L. *Increasing the utilization of applied research results* (final report to the National Institute of Mental Health). Los Angeles: Human Interaction Institute, 1971.

CHAPTER 9

FINDINGS AND CONCLUSIONS ON INTERPERSONAL SOCIAL MARKETING

A Brief Look Forward

Two key theoretical areas are the focus of attention in this high-intensity social marketing study: *Internal* versus *External* and *Authority* versus *Peer* diffusion agent effects. Previous literature exhibits varied and conflicting findings concerning which leadership types would most facilitate adoption and implementation of a new practice strategy. The underdeveloped state of knowledge led us to take an exploratory stance on this issue. We examined the relationships without positing specific hypotheses.

The approach to the analysis performed to examine the relationships may be visualized as shown in Figure 9.1. The different types of diffusion agents, relying primarily on a workshop medium of marketing, sought to promote use of a handbook containing professional innovations. The Depth of Utilization score yielded by the DU Scale is the indicator of handbook use and constitutes the dependent variable.

In this chapter we examine a series of contingent variables that may have an impact on utilization, such as the handbook package and the workshop. We also examine structural variables briefly.

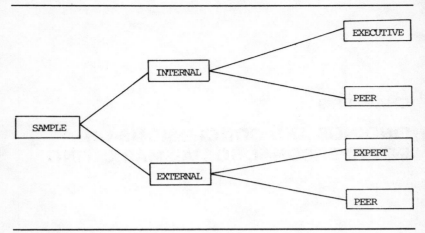

Figure 9.1

Internal Versus External Diffusion Agents

We have already noted that the disadvantages of one diffusion agent type appear to be the advantages of the other. Havelock (1970, pp. 47-50) says:

> [The] inside change agent . . . knows the system, . . . speaks the language, . . . understands the norms, . . . identifies with the system's needs and aspirations, . . . is a familiar figure. The insider also has these disadvantages. He lacks perspective, . . . may not have the special knowledge or skill, . . . may not have an adequate power base, . . . may have to live down his past failures, . . . may not have the independence of movement, . . . usually faces the difficult task of redefining his ongoing relationships with the other members of the system. The outsider has these advantages. He starts fresh, . . . is in a position to have perspective, . . . is independent, . . . is in a position to bring in something genuinely new. The outsider has these disadvantages. He is a stranger, [and] . . . may not "care enough."

Watson and Glaser (1965, p. 36) note:

> The outside advisor may be variously viewed as a troublemaker, as a knowledgeable specialist, or as a helpful friend. . . . When a top

management man takes the lead in making changes, he . . . runs risk. He depends upon others. . . . If the manager is brashly eager . . . he may get only tepid cooperation. If he is too impatient . . . he may incur resistance or even sabotage.

These two views are intended to reiterate the point we made earlier, namely, researchers are divided as to the effectiveness of internal and external change agents in relation to each other. We will attempt to address the issue of evaluating change agent type using the data gathered in our high-intensity marketing study.

Comparing the DU scores for internal versus external diffusion agents, mean internal scores (2.04) were higher than external scores (1.89). Using a threefold (low, medium, high) contingency table analysis, the differences approached but did not quite reach significance at the $p = .05$ level (both maximum likelihood and chi square significance levels were .07). Table 9.1 presents the contingency level for low, medium, and high scores. The directions in both the low and high group are in favor of the internal agent.

In addition to the DU scores, several other questionnaire items differentiated between internal and external diffusion agents. Staff who experienced internal leadership had more favorable responses at the .05 level or beyond on five items. The internally led workshop participants were more likely to indicate:

	chi square (p =)	maximum likelihood (p =)
The handbook helped the agency.	.02	.02
The workshop was adequate.	.00	.00
The workshop experience encouraged utilization of the handbook.	.03	.03
The workshop was informative.	.05	.04
The workshop fulfilled my expectations.	.00	.00

Even on items with no significant level of difference, the direction of response consistently favored the internally led workshops.

TABLE 9.1   Effectiveness of External Versus Internal Diffusion Agents

Diffusion Agent	Extent of Utilization		
	Low	Medium	High
Internal actual	55	55	62
(expected)	(58)	(62)	(52)
External actual	72	79	51
(expected)	(69)	(72)	(61)

NOTE: $\chi^2 = .072$;   maximum likelihood = .072.

EFFECTS OF PERSONAL ATTRIBUTES OF PARTICIPANTS

It seemed to us useful to determine whether characteristics of participants were related to their reaction to internal or external diffusion agents. Relating DU score to diffusion agent types, we discovered the following groups were significantly (.05 level or beyond) motivated by internal agents:

	chi square (p =)	maximum likelihood (p =)
those with less than one year on this job	.04	.04
moderate years of experience in the human service field	.02	.02
professionally identified with psychology or psychiatry	.00	.00
relatively higher proportion of real time spent in research tasks	.04	.04

None of the other personal attributes of participants was significant as related to internal/external differences. Those signaling differences all favored the internal agent and included age, sex, percentage of time spent in administration, percentage of time spent in supervision, direct service roles, and community work roles.

TABLE 9.2 Effectiveness of External Versus Internal Diffusion Agents: CMHCs

	Extent of Utilization		
Diffusion Agent	Low	Medium	High
Internal actual	39	28	52
(expected)	(39)	(39)	(41)
External actual	49	60	41
(expected)	(49)	(49)	(52)

NOTE: $\chi^2 = .005$; maximum likelihood = .005.

CMHC Versus FSAA

As there were some clear group differences in evidence, this suggested an examination of whether the general internal/external diffusion agent pattern we had found in the aggregated agency data continued to hold when we examined CMHCs and FSAAs separately. The DU scores were as follows:

	internal leadership	external leadership
Total sample	2.04	1.89
CMHCs	2.11	1.95
FSAAs	1.89	1.75

Using the threefold (high, medium, low) contingency table analysis plan, differences in DU scores were significant for CMHCs and not for FSAAs. Table 9.2 presents the contingency table for CMHC data; Table 9.3 is the contingency table for FSAAs. Although the FSAA data are not significant, the directionality is consistent with the other findings. Note that the FSAA sample is considerably smaller than the CMHC sample.

GROUP COMPOSITION: A POTENTIAL BIASING FACTOR

The trend of the data ran in a direction favoring the internal diffusion agent as a stimulus for utilization. The matter was not clear-cut, however. Workshop participants within the sample

TABLE 9.3   Effectiveness of External Versus Internal Diffusion
Agents: FSAAs

	Extent of Utilization		
Diffusion Agent	Low	Medium	High
Internal actual	16	27	10
(expected)	(20)	(23)	(10)
External actual	23	19	10
(expected)	(19)	(23)	(10)

NOTE: χ^2 = .27; maximum likelihood = .27.

agencies were selected autonomously by the agencies in varied
ways by the agency contact persons. Though our sampling
controls were geared to agency type and geographic considerations, we could not and did not control the characteristics and
attributes of the workshop participants. We considered the
possibility, therefore, that differential composition of workshop
membership, rather than the experimental independent variable,
may have influenced the results.

We examined the membership of workshops to determine
whether there were significant differences among different
workshops. In examining participant characteristics and a large
number of structural variables, there were few significant differences between internal/external samples that were related to
differences in DU scores. No participant variable showed problematic differences. Several agency background variables, however, were cause for concern.[1]

When looking at the total picture, we found no definitive
effects that could be said to have biased the findings in a
particular direction. While the picture is complex and open to
differing interpretations, an analysis of all possible variables
available to us gave us no clear reason to believe that contingent
intervening variables explained our basic findings.

INTERNAL VERSUS EXTERNAL DIFFUSION: CONCLUSIONS

Overall, the internal agent tended to evoke both more positive reactions from participants and a higher level of utilization.

The fact that some of the analyses did not yield significant differences leads to a cautious interpretation. The mixed composition of groups in the sample and counter tendencies within different sample subgroups also signal a note of caution. The consistency of the trend in favor of internal agents, however, is impressive. We interpret the findings to suggest greater effectiveness of internal agents in marketing professional innovations through workshops. At the same time, we feel that further research is necessary. Such research may also indicate contingent variables that may have an influence on the results. Indeed, additional work conducted in this study (and that we shall report shortly) suggests one such contingency that needs to be considered: the nature of the innovation or product being diffused.

Authority Versus Peer Diffusion Agents

The questions to be answered in this analysis are: Do authority-initiated changes and peer-initiated changes differ in their effectiveness? Did either approach evoke a more favorable response to the handbook and greater subsequent utilization of innovative professional practices? As we indicated earlier, the research literature has reached conflicting conclusions concerning the effectiveness of authority- versus peer-initiated change.

Havelock and Havelock (1973, p. 20) solicited reactions to certain questions about change agent success and obtained unanimous agreement that "effective dissemination and utilization are facilitated by informal opinion leaders." Hage and Dewar (1971), in a 1964-1966 study, found that hierarchy of authority was negatively related to program innovation.

On the other hand, some authors stress the importance of authority-initiated change. Zaltman et al. (1973, pp. 80-81) state that "decision by authority . . . can be made within a relatively short period of time."

Becker (1970, p. 281) states that "earliest adopters . . . were found to be individuals with high relative centrality." Thus we see that scholars and researchers on each side of this issue muster reasonable evidence and/or arguments to buttress their hypotheses.

The approach to the analysis was to compare participant responses on the questionnaire for those experiencing an authority diffusion agent with those experiencing a peer agent. Dependent variables obtained from the questionnaires that were used to detect differences between authority and peer influences included the DU score and a series of attitudinal items.

Of 28 variables examined from the follow-up questionnaire, only 1, "reaction to the handbook," with both chi square and maximum likelihood probability levels of .04, indicated a significant degree of difference between workshop participants attending authority- or peer-led workshops. DU scores were likewise identical, 1.96, for both the authority and peer treatments. Table 9.4 is the contingency table of expected versus actual results on this handbook reaction variable.

Table 9.4 indicates that those respondents from the *authority* treatments had a more favorable reaction to the handbook than those respondents from the peer treatments. Thus executive staff members or outside experts seemed to leave participants with a more favorable view of the handbook, but this did not eventuate in differences in the actual *use* of the handbook.

The absence of difference in authority or peer effects was demonstrated in both the CMHC and FSAA subsamples. Mean DU scores were as follows:

	CMHCs	FSAAs
Authority	2.04	1.82
Peer	2.01	1.82

Differences were not found to approach significant levels.

GROUP COMPOSITION: A POTENTIALLY BIASING FACTOR

Again, we were concerned about the characteristics of participant samples and of agency structural variables as possible factors influencing the results. An underrepresentation of prac-

TABLE 9.4   Reactions to the Handbook

| | Reactions | | |
Diffusion Agent	Favorable	Less Favorable	Unfavorable
Internal actual	63	48	49
(external)	(53)	(52)	(54)
External actual	54	69	74
(external)	(65)	(65)	(67)

NOTE: χ^2 = .04; maximum likelihood = .04.

titioner or agency factors, for example, for either the authority or peer treatments, if related to high utilization, could have dissipated favorable results for one or the other of the treatment groups. Table 9.5 gives the range of variables we examined to determine factors that might influence the direction of our results.

There are a number of significant differences in composition between authority and peer samples. Only those differences that had been found to be related to utilization will be discussed.

As Table 9.6 demonstrates, the peer sample had a higher proportion of respondents from NIMH agencies. As an NIMH affiliation was positively related to utilization, this uneven distribution could have decreased the effect of the authority agent while increasing the positive effect of the peer agent.

PARTICIPANT CHARACTERISTICS

There were no significant differences between authority and peer samples regarding participant characteristics that were additionally related to utilization.

Structural Factors

Although there were six variables that were significantly different for the authority versus peer treatments, only one of these, "percentage of professional employees in 'other' cate-

TABLE 9.5 Potentially Biasing Variables

Variable	Maximum Likelihood (p =)	Chi Square (p =)
Delivery system	.035*	.035*
Participant Characteristics		
Age	.00*	.00*
Sex	.01*	.01*
Educational degree	.08	.08
Time in job	.00*	.00*
Administrative role (% time)	.19	.20
Supervisory role (% time)	.82	.82
Direct service role (% time)	.41	.41
Community work role (% time)	.32	.32
Research (% time)	.27	.27
Human service employment (length of time)	.00*	.00*
Professional identity (psychology, psychiatry, social work, nursing)	.06	.06
Structural Characteristics		
Attitudes of director:		
Decision-making style	.00*	.00*
receptivity to ideas	.00*	.00*
community orientation	.00*	.00*
Total expenditures	.66	.66
% staff in minority groups	.11	.11
Population services	.03*	.03*
No. of Professional Employees	.68	.68
No. of Full-Time Social Workers	.34	.33
% social workers (full and part time)	.88	.88
Professional employees in other positions	.54	.54
Nongraduate social work practitioners	.00*	.00*
% nongraduate social workers relative to total staff	.00*	.00*
Salary and expenditures	.68	.68
% salary in relation to total expenditures	.67	.67
% government income	.00*	.00*
Ratio staff to 100,000 population	.97	.97
% professional employees in auxilliary positions	.00*	.00*

*Statistically significant.

TABLE 9.6 Rate of Response, by Delivery System and Diffusion Agent Type

Service Delivery System	Diffusion Agent	
	Authority	Peer
NIMH actual	111	158
(expected)	(120)	(149)
FSAA actual	56	49
(expected	(47)	(58)

NOTE: $\chi^2 = .04$; maximum likelihood = .04.

gories relative to all staff," was previously found to be related to utilization. The contingency table for this variable is Table 9.7.

In this case, authority respondents came from agencies with a higher percentage of "other" professionals. As the proportion of "other" professionals had been found to be positively associated with utilization, this overrepresentation of "other" professionals could have added a positive effect to the authority group while decreasing the peer agent effects.

In summary, after examining all available variables, only two utilization-relevant variables were found to have a significant difference in relation to authority versus peer treatments: delivery system and percentage of professional employees in other categories. As these results are inconclusive regarding directionality, however, little can actually be concluded.

AUTHORITY VERSUS PEER DIFFUSION: CONCLUSIONS

Unlike internal versus external influences, our data suggest that it makes little difference whether the diffusion agent is an authority figure (member of the executive staff, outside expert) or some type of staff peer (from within the agency or outside). Follow-up utilization appears to be about the same for both types of agents. There is little difference with regard to attitudinal effects for these different diffusion/marketing types.

TABLE 9.7   Professional Employees in "Other" Categories Relative to All Staff

% of Professional Employees in "Other" Categories	Diffusion Agent	
	Authority	Peer
0 actual	16	37
(expected)	(20)	(33)
1-7 actual	34	82
(expected)	(44)	(72)
8+ actual	57	53
(expected)	(42)	(68)

NOTE: χ^2 = .00; maximum likelihood = .00.

Combined Effects of Status and Locus

In the previous analysis we learned that status level (authority versus peer) is not a critical factor with regard to subsequent utilization, but that location inside or outside the organization may be. The next question is whether a given status level *and* location is more conducive to utilization than some other combination of the two. Figure 9.2 conceptualizes the issue. Four different combined treatments are depicted within this framework. Our analysis task is to determine whether DU scores were different among these various cells.

We found that this variable was not significant in the contingency table analysis and ranked low to moderate in the multiple classification and discriminant analyses. Table 9.8 is the contingency table for the DU scores. In no case do they approach significance.

No combined approach, apparently, stands out as an optimal diffusion agent's platform in marketing professional innovations. We are left only with the earlier, broader generalization that internal, compared to external, agents are perhaps more likely to induce implementation of innovative professional practices within agencies.

| | Locus | |
	Inside	Outside
Authority	1 inside authority	3 outside authority
Status Level		
Peer	inside peer 2	outside peer 4

Figure 9.2: Status Versus Locus

Diffusion Agent Type and
Immediate Participant Reactions

The analysis has thus far been concerned with the results of the subsequent follow-up investigation regarding handbook utilization, an investigation conducted several months after workshops were held. A question to consider is whether immediate reactions following the workshop experience would be consistent with the longer-range findings. The research question would be as follows: If participant reactions to different types of agents were gauged at the conclusion of the workshop, would they prefer the same type of agents who were shown in the later work to have fostered a greater degree of handbook utilization?

At the conclusion of the workshop sessions, all participants were asked to fill out a short "reactionnaire," giving their impressions and assessment of the workshop experience. They also had completed a registration form giving basic personal background information, identifying themselves and their agencies. Responses were obtained at workshops from 531 participants, representing 37 agencies. The format and items on the reactionnaire are indicated in Figure 9.3, with code names for items in brackets.

TABLE 9.8   Status-Locus Contingency Table—Depth of Utilization

Treatment		Extent of Utilization		
		Low	Medium	High
1	actual	27	28	36
	(expected)	(31)	(33)	(27)
2	actual	28	27	26
	(expected)	(28)	(29)	(24)
3	actual	30	31	15
	(expected)	(26)	(27)	(23)
4	actual	42	48	36
	(expected)	(43)	(45)	(38)

NOTE: x^2 = .27; maximum likelihood = .27.

The format of the reactionnaire is similar to a Likert scale. It uses an ordinal response scale with assigned scores of 1 to 5, corresponding to "strongly agree," "agree," "neutral," "disagree," and "strongly disagree."

There were eight independent nominal variables used to record personal attribute features and design factors. These variables were obtained in part from the registration form. Six specific questions, used to measure the practitioners' responses to the workshop, were the dependent variables.

Workshop participants evaluated the workshop in a strongly favorable direction. These uniform results made selection of appropriate analysis procedures more difficult. The character of the responses is indicated in Table 9.9.

The staff had operationalized the workshop format through a series of trials to arrive at a format that would be conducive to utilization. It is apparent that this was successful. It was so successful, in fact, that it served as an impediment to analysis because of insufficient variance of participant response.

All variables from the reactionnaires were categorical in nature. The descriptive background items were nominal variables, while the reactionnaire attitudinal questions were ordinal. This categorical nature of the data had strong influence on the selection of a contingency table type of analysis that is the most

	Strongly Agree	Agree	Neutral	Disagree	Strongly Disagree
The workshop helped me to understand the concepts in the handbook. [UNDERSTAND]	_____	_____	_____	_____	_____
The workshop helped me to be able to apply the handbook in my practice. [APPLY]	_____	_____	_____	_____	_____
The content of the workshop was clear and understandable. [CLEAR]	_____	_____	_____	_____	_____
The content was applicable to my work. [APPLICABILITY]	_____	_____	_____	_____	_____
The presentation of the workshop was effective. [EFFECTIVENESS]	_____	_____	_____	_____	_____
The workshop met my expectations and objectives. [EXPECTATION]	_____	_____	_____	_____	_____

General Comments (suggestions, criticisms, highlights, etc.)

Figure 9.3: Reactionnaire

appropriate for this type of data. As before, the chi square and maximum likelihood statistics were used for data interpretation.

In order to arrive at a sufficient cell size, because of the high degree of workshop favorableness, we decided to collapse each ordinal scale reporting workshop attitudes to increase the number of responses per cell in the contingency tables. "Strongly agree" (SA) and "agree" (A) remained separate categories,

TABLE 9.9   Reactionnaire Results

| | Reactionnaire Categories | | | | | | | | | | | | |
| | Understand | | Apply | | Clear | | Applica-bility | | Effective-ness | | Expecta-tion | | Total | |
	No.	%	No.	%	No.	%	No.	%	No.	%	No.	%	No.	%
Strongly agree/ agree	429	91.4	350	75.1	412	88.0	389	83.3	401	86.1	299	65.1	2280	81.5
Neutral/ disagree/ strongly disagree	40	8.5	116	24.9	56	12.0	78	16.7	65	13.9	160	34.9	515	18.5

because they already had sufficient response levels. "Neutral," "disagree," and "strongly disagree" were combined to form one category (NDSD), because, individually, they did not have sufficient response levels. This category indicates those "less favorable." When this was done only two cells, Apply ("The workshop helped me to be able to apply the Handbook in my practice") and Expectation ("The workshop met my expectations and objectives") were significant at the .05 level or beyond.

These findings suggest that, with respect to Apply, having an external agent appears to be associated with practitioners feeling that workshops helped them apply the handbook to their practice. With respect to Expectation, external authority agents received more favorable responses than we had expected.

The results of the reactionnaire study indicate that external agent workshops evoked differential and stronger responses with regard to specific items, with the external expert seemingly in the most favored position. Practitioners felt that external diffusion agents, whether experts or peers, helped them apply the concepts of the handbook to their practice. In addition, they felt that external experts contributed to the workshop's meeting their expectations and objectives.

Diffusion Agent Type and Nature of Innovation Product

The foregoing has presented the basic data that were generated by the study regarding the questions being investigated. A first impression may be that there is some conflict or inconsistency within the findings. Internal agents tended to produce more favorable effects in the follow-up Depth of Utilization study. External agents tended to produce more favorable reactionnaire responses immediately following the workshop experience.

This inconsistency is explainable when we look at the kinds of data the two different instruments were gathering. The *reactionnaire* recorded feelings and attitudes of participants.

Apparently, external agents were able to evoke stronger, more favorable immediate reactions than were indigenous colleagues and administrators with whom participants were familiar. The *DU instrument* focused primarily on actual behavior of participants in implementing the innovative practice techniques being diffused. It would seem that internal agents are better able to bring about long-term implemental activity.

This seeming paradox is not unduly perplexing. External agents, it might be inferred, are better able to "stir things up" in the immediate situation. They are fresh to the organizational environs, may come with an aura of professional respectability or acclaim, and can create a sense of excitement relating to bringing something new. They hint at a promise of better, locally unknown solutions to existing problems. The external agent may provoke greater attention at the time of the workshop and leave people with a sense of having participated in a "happening."

The internal agent, however, remains in the organizational environment. He or she is on the premises to remind people of the innovation in person, to encourage them to perform, to offer advice or concrete assistance in moving ahead with implementation. Indeed, this individual's very presence in a passive role may remind people of the workshop and/or the handbook. That presence may reinforce any tendencies they might have to go ahead (or create guilt, if they do not).

The question of whether an internal or external diffusion agent is "better" in fostering utilization of innovative ideas and techniques depends, in part, on the nature of the innovation and the objective. If the objective is to convey a new idea, to have people obtain a flash of insight, or to use a discrete, simple innovation immediately, then the outside agent (especially an "expert") may have a more favorable effect. If the innovation is rather complex and requires sustained implemental behavior over time, then the inside agent, perhaps, would be preferable. The internal agent persists in the situation and can continue to motivate, explain, and assist as the complicated innovation is operationalized and internalized as a practice technique.

These distinctions seem to have been implicated in the variations in findings uncovered in this marketing study. It can be inferred from this discussion that the optimal arrangement for complex innovation would be a collaborative team made up of internal and external members. The external person can maximize attention and impact in the conveying phase; the internal person can maximize follow through in the implemental phase.

Demonstrations of successful internal/external teams have been presented in the literature (for example, see Gluckstern & Packard, 1977). Havelock (1973, p. 53) states the general proposition as follows:

> In order to capitalize on the advantages and avoid the problems of both insider and outsider, many experienced change agents have suggested that the best solution is a "change agent team" in which both insiders and outsiders work together.... Any selection of members for the inside-outside team should try to maximize the strengths of both positions in the service of innovation.

There is further support for the mixed team position from Argyris (1974), who feels that internally generated decisions need external inputs to move them toward organizational action. The internal/external team option may be viewed in terms of marketing theories that call for a "promotional mix" in developing diffusion approaches.

Our references concerning the nature of the innovation and internal/external agent considerations are substantiated theoretically in the literature of innovation diffusion. In addressing that literature, we draw largely on the work of Rogers and Shoemaker (1971) and Zaltman et al. (1973), who have completed extensive reviews and syntheses of this literature in their professionally recognized books. We draw also upon a previous report of the Community Intervention Project in which a similar review was undertaken (Rothman, 1974).

Zaltman et al. (1973) indicate that innovations have different characteristics. They talk about programmed and unprogrammed innovations and include other aspects as well. Both

Zaltman et al. and Rogers and Shoemaker specifically include complexity as an aspect of innovations, indicating that the more complex the innovation, the more difficult or uncertain the adoption. Rogers and Shoemaker (1971, p. 154) define complexity as

> the degree to which an innovation is perceived as relatively difficult to understand and use. Any new idea may be classified on the complexity-simplicity continuum.

The role of a change agent in working through the complexity dimension with a target system is suggested in the CIP publication (Rothman, 1974, p. 445):

> In order to maximize the adoption rate of an innovation, the practitioner should formulate the innovation at a level of complexity which can be accommodated by a target system.... The issue of complexity must be viewed in the framework of the system's perception.... As much as possible, the practitioner should explain the innovation in simple or familiar terms.

Indeed, Rogers and Shoemaker (1971) point out, adoption rates may be a function of the sheer amount of time and energy devoted by a change agent to the innovative task. They state: "Change agent success is related to the extent of change agent efforts" (p. 233). They cite research indicating that change agent activity is not as influential in the *early* stage. After the innovation has been institutionalized during the critical middle stage, it may gain momentum under its own impetus; and the agent can again reduce the extent of his or her activity. The observations by Rogers and Shoemaker further explain the potential beneficial effect of the indigenous agent who remains in the situation for a time as compared to the expert who introduces a new idea and then is gone.

The advantages of the internal agent are additionally explicated by Rogers and Shoemaker through the use of the term "homophily," the degree to which interacting individuals are similar in certain attributes. According to these authors, more effective communication takes place when the source and the receiver have attributes in common:

> A homophilous dyad share common meanings and interests; they are better able to empathize with each other because the other's role is similar [Rogers & Shoemaker, 1971, p. 241].

Clearly, the internal agent is more likely to meet the homophily criterion. The factor with attitudes and norms within the organization relates to another generalization from the CIP report. This was stated as follows:

> The rate of adoption of an innovation is directly related to the extent to which it is diffused in a manner compatible with the target system's norms, values, and customs. Innovations with a compatible diffusion process will have a higher adoption rate than innovations with an incompatible process [Rothman, 1974, p. 446].

The internal agent stands in an advantageous position in this connection. This notion is related in part also to another CIP generalization, which states that an innovation is more likely to be adopted when the target group perceives internal support for the new idea within its own relevant system. The indigenous agent represents and conveys a beginning of such internal support. Zaltman et al. (1973, p. 40) cite research showing that when a set of innovations carried out in industry was traced back, 77 percent of the innovations were found to have originated *within* the firm *rather than outside.*

Understanding of our findings is further facilitated by viewing innovation adoption as a *process* that unfolds over time, rather than as a discrete event. Both Rogers and Shoemaker and Zaltman et al. describe aspects of adoption, although in somewhat different language. Zaltman et al. refer to an "initiation stage" and a later "implementation stage," pointing out different process characteristics in each. Initiation involves knowledge awareness, requiring the communication and absorption of information. The implementation stage is viewed as including an initial trial substage, followed by a continued, sustained carrying-out substage. Zaltman et al. (1973, p. 71) point out the importance of feedback in an adoptive-coping capacity during implementation: "Feedback serves the purpose of guiding and controlling the actual performance of the process." The crucial place, potentially, of an internal agent in this connection is evident.

Rogers and Shoemaker address the same general issue in terms of evaluation. They feel that one of the key functions of a change agent is to assist his or her client group to assess the impact of an innovation as it is carried out: "A change agent's success is positively related to his efforts in increasing his clients' ability to evaluate innovations" (p. 247). Rogers and Shoemaker point out several features of innovations that, if evaluated favorably, can facilitate adoption; for example, perceived relative advantage of the innovation compared to the existing situation, and the degree to which it is seen to be compatible with client needs.

Zaltman et al. list a series of psychological factors related to adoption that are, presumably, amenable to evaluation. These include motivation, perception, attitude, need for legitimation, confidence to undertake a trial use, and so on. All of these areas may require sustained and close support through various stages of the adoption process.

Rogers and Shoemaker see the adoption process as requiring the potential user of an innovation to pass through a series of decisions *over time*. The decisional context is different at different stages:

> Knowing about an innovation is often quite a different matter from using the idea. Most individuals know about many innovations which they have not adopted. Why? One reason is because the individual knows about the new idea but does not regard it as relevant to his situation, as potentially useful. Therefore, attitudes toward an innovation frequently intervene between the knowledge and decision functions. In other words, the individual's attitudes or beliefs about the innovation have much to say about his passage through the decision process [Rogers & Shoemaker, 1971, p. 108].

This difference between knowing and using reflects in a certain sense two different stages at which our instruments tested respondents. Writing from a marketing perspective, Shaw (1967) views the issue in terms of acceptance of new products. He highlights the complexity of gaining such acceptance, and the need for close follow-up in the following passage:

> In the study of diffusion of innovations it might be helpful to think of the adoption process as consisting of five distinct but related stages. Behavioral scientists conceptualize this process of being composed of the awareness, interest, evaluation, trial and adoption or rejection stages.
>
> Behavioral science research also suggests that the speed of acceptance or failure of an innovation is closely related to the ability of the consumer to perceive and evaluate its superiorities. Not only economic advantage, but such product attributes as compatibility, complexity, divisibility, and communicability are important to the early adopters [Shaw, 1974, p. 274].

We have explained the results we obtained in part, but another aspect still needs to be examined. The foregoing helps clarify why the internal agent who had a continuing role in the agency may have contributed to a higher rate of utilization. What, though, accounts for the more positive immediate reaction to the external expert? The diffusion literature is not a source of theoretical enlightenment on this issue. However, research on attitude change and persuasion seems to offer a small measure of assistance.

Several writers in the field point to credibility of the communicator as a significant variable in influencing attitudes. Cohen (1964, p. 29) summarizes a range of relevant research:

> Variations in the credibility of the communicator do indeed determine variations in attitude change: the greater the trustworthiness or expertness (expertise? "expert" status?), the greater the change toward the position advocated by the communicator.

Abelson (1959) isolates and explains these same two factors in regard to credibility. It is his position that when an audience decides a communicator lacks credibility, the members of that audience (1) do not pay attention to him or her, and thus do not "hear" the message, and/or (2) are not motivated to comply with the direction of the message. Bettinghaus (1968, p. 109) attaches different labels to these terms ("safety" for trustworthiness, "qualification" or "competence" for expertness) and states that credibility is not a fixed or absolute characteristic of a given communicator:

> The amount of credibility that an individual is seen to have is a function of who the receiver is, what the topic is, and what the situation is.

The twofold conceptual formulation can be used in our marketing study in a heuristic fashion. We may assume that the outside expert would be rated high on expertise or qualification by workshop participants. The familiar indigenous workshop leader might be assumed to be rated high on trustworthiness or safety.

It seems reasonable to assume that during the workshop presentation the external person could acquire an increment in trustworthiness level because of the manner of presentation, how questions are answered, and interaction with participants before and after the workshop sessions and during the breaks. The outside person thus is in a position to add on to one of the two components of credibility. It is less likely that the insider will acquire an equivalent increment in expertness on the basis of having attended one training session regarding the use of the handbook. The outsider, therefore, is in a position potentially to acquire a greater mass of credibility. In addition, the outsider may be able to bring forth greater attention in the one-session workshop situation on the basis of novelty.

Opinion change research also suggests that the impact of the credibility of the communicator fades over time:

> A high credibility source may be important if the persuasion attempt is designed to get immediate results (signing a petition, starting a riot, taking a vote). However, if the aim of persuasion is long term,

then the believability of the communicator may not be such a crucial issue [Abelson, 1959, p. 75].

In that case, the kinds of activities in which the internal agent on the scene is able to engage, in terms of interpretation, encouragement, and evaluation, may make a discernible difference with regard to more long-term utilization behavior.

These theoretical notes are suggestive and leave much room for additional research and analysis. They do, however, go some of the way in helping to explain the findings and in giving reason to believe that our concluding hypothesis is plausible. Further systematic research regarding the specific hypothesis provides the best avenue for definite substantiation.

Findings: Factors Associated
with High Utilization

In the previous section we discussed findings related to the primary theoretical issues we had undertaken to examine. During the course of our study, data were accumulated with respect to a range of additional variables and their relationship to the extent of adoption or utilization of innovative practice techniques. In this section we will review that set of data. Basically, we will consider DU score as the dependent variable and relate it to factors under such categories as Personal Characteristics of Respondents, Reactions of Participants to the Workshop Experience and to the Handbook, Factors that Inhibited Completion of a Guideline, and the Administrative Style and Orientation of the Agency Executive.

Data acquired for this segment of the high-intensity social marketing study were obtained from the three-month follow-up questionnaire, from record keeping, and from interviews with national and regional directors of NIMH and FSAA, who rated agency directors. The questionnaire was used for recording practitioners' personal or demographic features, retrospective reactions to the experience, experiences in using the handbook, factors preventing guideline implementation, and levels of utilization. In addition, the project record-keeping system was used for obtaining treatment and design factors for each respondent, such as region and city, workshop leader, and so forth. Finally, interviews with national and regional directors of NIMH and FSAA were used for acquiring an indication of the decision-making style, receptivity to innovations, and community orientation for agency administrators involved in the high-intensity study.

In analyzing the data, several different techniques were used in conjunction with one another. First, contingency tables were employed to provide a descriptive profile of independent variables in relation to the DU dependent variable. Statistical procedures associated with contingency tables (maximum likelihood and chi square) permitted the determination of those variables that indicated a significant degree of relationship with DU.

A second procedure we used, multiple classification analysis (MCA) is primarily a technique for examining interrelationships between the independent variables and dependent variables (Andrews, 1973). An important function of this technique, however, is that it permits the *ranking* of independent variables according to the degree to which each is related to Depth of Utilization.

We also used discriminant analysis to describe previously identified groups of individuals for purposes of deciding whether or not the groups were, in fact, distinguishable. The discriminant functions generated during the analysis can also be used to classify individuals whose group membership is unknown. A population is described by a grouping variable (DU) and a set of discriminating variables (treatment, design, demographic and attitudinal variables, and so on). A model can be developed in terms of intergroup distances, misclassification rates, and the contribution of each variable to the discrimination. A ranking can be made concerning the degree to which each variable contributes to the discriminant function.

Our analysis, then, sought to indicate which variables were significantly related to DU, both individually and in relation to other independent variables. Two different statistical procedures having the capability of performing such a function were used, in addition to the contingency table analyses, for determining independent-dependent variable relationships.

Table 9.10 lists all variables originally in the study design and their designation according to the three analysis procedures. It also indicates an overall ranking of variables in relation to impact on utilization. This overall rank was determined by appraising the full display of the data. As contingency tables were calculated for each variable, those results carried the most weight. Contingency tables, too, give a clear and explicit significance measure and a salient picture of the distribution and trends, if any. The MCA and discriminant analysis (DA) tests are more subjective in nature, for they attempt to rank variables according to their relative prediction strength for future situations. For technical reasons, many variables that are similar in nature must be excluded. Hence there is an obvious absence of some variables in the rankings that are too closely associated with other variables. Because of the technical aspects of the procedures, MCA rankings were obtained for only 12 variables, while DA rankings go up to 17 variables. Most variables not included in either ranking were eliminated for either statistical or technical reasons, such as overlap, close association with other variables, and so on.

Ultimately, the final rankings were based upon significance in the contingency tables and a relatively high rank as a predictor of utilization in both the MCA and DA. If a variable was only extant in one of the two (MCA or DA), its final rank was reduced. The overall ranking was based on consensus judgments among the three members of our data processing research staff who had primary responsibility for this aspect of the analysis. Informed judgment, then, interacted with empirical data in arriving at conclusions. Significance on the contingency tables was a prerequisite for consideration in the final rankings. In this table the variables rated among the top ten are shown in italics. For those not so rated, but where significant differences were found, the direction of the difference is indicated. Direction of

(text continues on page 210)

TABLE 9.10 High-Intensity Variables and Rankings on Utilization Impact

Variable	Direction of Relationship	Rankings		
		MCA	DA	Overall
A. Treatment				
Four different combinations of location and status	(The internal/executive treatment yielded relatively more utilization; the external/expert yielded relatively less utilization.)	7	16	
B. General Design Factors				
Delivery systems: CMHC–FSAA	*CMHC respondents had a higher utilization rate than FSAA respondents.*	5		7
Specific agencies				
Different cities				
Different regions	Difficult to delineate specific regional differences.		6	
Staff workshop leaders				
C. Participant Demographics				
Age				
Sex				
Education (degree)				
Length of time in present job				
% time in administrative duties				

% time in supervisory duties				
* % time in direct services	*Those less in direct services were more likely to be higher utilizers.*	9	14	8
% time in community work	(Those with more time in community work were more likely to be higher utilizers.)	3	9	
% time in research				
Years of experience in the human service field				
Professional identity				
D. Workshop Involvement and Reactions				
Participated in workshop				
*Found workshop adequate	Those who found the workshop adequate were more likely to be medium to high utilizers.			
*Workshop encouraged/ discouraged utilization	Those who thought the workshop encouraged utilization were more likely to be high utilizers.			
*Workshop helped apply concepts to practice	*Those who felt the workshop helped apply concepts to practice were more likely to be high utilizers.*	2	5	4
Workshop helped to understand concepts				
*Workshop fulfilled expectations	Those who felt the workshop fulfilled their expectations were more likely to be high utilizers.			

(continued)

TABLE 9.10 Continued

*Workshop was informative	Those who felt the workshop was "very" informative were more likely to be high utilizers; "somewhat" were medium; "not" were low utilizers.
	12
Change in the content of the workshop was necessary	
*Change in the presentation of the workshop was necessary	Those who saw a change in the presentation of the workshop as necessary in encouraging utilization were more likely to be high utilizers.
	8
	9
*Change in the design of the workshop was necessary	Those who thought a change in workshop necessary for encouraging utilization were more likely to be high utilizers.
	4
	6
E. Handbook Experiences and Reactions	
*Applicable to the work of the agency	As applicability of the handbook to the agency increases, utilization increases.
	11
*Applicable to job	As applicability to job increases, utilization also increases.
*Handbook not too technical	Those who "strongly agreed" were high utilizers; "agreed" were medium; "disagreed" were low utilizers.

*Reaction to handbook	As one's reaction to the handbook became more favorable, utilization rate rose.		15	1
*Handbook encouraged/discouraged utilization	*Those who thought the handbook encouraged implementation of a guideline were more likely to be high utilizers.*	1	4	1
*Will refer back to handbook	*Those who said they would refer back to the handbook were more likely to be medium to high utilizers.*		1	2
*Filled out an initial log	Those who filled out an initial log were more likely to be higher utilizers.		7	
*Applied concepts without filling out an initial log	*Those who applied the concepts without filling out an initial log were more likely to be high utilizers.*		2	5
*Effect of current agency situation on use of handbook	Those who said agency effects "helped" were more likely to be high utilizers; those who said it did not help were more likely to be low utilizers.		13	3
*Previous activity similar to handbook activity	*Those who indicated previous, similar activity were more likely to be high utilizers; those who answered "no" were more likely to be medium or low utilizers.*	6	3	3
F. Factors Preventing Completion of a Guideline				
*Time	Those who indicated that "time" was a preventing factor were more likely to be high utilizers.			

(continued)

TABLE 9.10 Continued

Money		
*Not related to job role	10	10
	Those who indicated that the guideline was not related to their job role were more likely to be lower utilizers than those who did not so indicate.	
Insufficient assistance given in use of the handbook		
Personal factors		
Lack of administrative support		
Lack of collegial support		
Lack of supervisory support		
More assistance needed in use of the handbook		
More assistance needed in the agency		

G. Structural Variables

Centrality of decision making by agency director	(Where the director used a more decentralized decision-making style, utilization rates were higher.)	11	17
Receptivity to outside ideas by agency director	(Where the director was highly receptive to outside ideas, utilization rates were higher.)	12	
Community orientation and commitment by agency director	(Where directors were more community oriented, utilization rates were slightly higher.)	8	

*Significant at the .05 level.

difference is also indicated in parentheses for those variables that were not found to be significant but achieved a ranking in the MCA or DA procedures. Thus three different levels of weighting are indicated in the direction column. Highest weighted items are shown in italics. Items written in but not in italics indicate a low weighting. Items with no directionality written in are considered inert in relation to variations in utilization. This is, of necessity, a complex table, not easily read or digested. The following discussion pinpoints its salient conclusions.

It is interesting to note that personal characteristics of participants did not constitute a particularly strong factor. Age, sex, or experience did not seem to predict an inclination to utilize the handbook. Only percentage of time spent in certain job-related functions, particularly in direct service, seemed to affect predilection to use the handbook. This aspect of job relatedness emerges recurrently in the data and appears to be a highly relevant variable.

The most potent factor in fostering utilization appears to be the *handbook* itself. Both because of the number of subitems appearing as significant and because the top two items in the overall ranking pertain to the handbook, this factor must be considered of prime importance as a spur to utilization. In particular, an indication by a respondent that the handbook encouraged utilization, or that he or she would refer back to the handbook in the future, signified potential utilization. Also of significance was an indication that the handbook was applicable to one's job or agency or the impression that it would have favorable effects in the agency currently or in the future.

The role of packaging is well recognized in the marketing field. According to Newman (1957, p. 100), the product can be viewed as a "symbol by virtue of its form, size, color, and functions. Its significance as a symbol varies according to how much it is associated with individual needs." DeLozier (1976, p. 175) underlines the matter as follows: "The most important component of the product as a communication is the package." Packaging is viewed as performing a number of functions, among them containing and providing physical protection for the product, promoting its purchase or utilization, and providing convenience in utilization (Boone & Kurtz, 1977). Despite its emphasis on symbol and form, the fundamental attribute of packaging is meeting needs or fulfilling functions. To put it another way, "The product must deliver what the package promises" (DeLozier, 1976, p. 176). Apparently, in the high-intensity study there was a blending of product, package, and perceived utility.

Our data suggest that in attempting to promote an innovative program or technique, special attention should be given to the packaging or structuring of the medium of transmission. The results of this study imply that overriding attention and care should be paid to this element. Consumer marketing, of course, has devoted much thought, time, and money to the packaging of a product. These results suggest that the packaging of a social product is equally important.

Next in importance seems to be the workshop that introduces the handbook and trains and motivates participants in its use. A large number of the items that were significant were workshop related, including three of the ten overall highest rankings. Again, a job-related item ranked fourth ("The workshop helped me apply the handbook to my practice"). Other aspects of the workshop that affected utilization were its design, an agency situation permitting it to be beneficially conducted and encouraging utilization, and the fact that it was informative and fulfilled the participants' expectations. Thus one lesson appears to be that training experiences should be designed with care and sensitivity. A second lesson is that the potential of marketing channels should be maximized. The latter lesson is essential to effective diffusion; the former is crucial to utilization.

A grouping of specific agency- and job-relevant items cluster together as of high importance; for example, whether the innovative practice tool is related to one's job, whether the participant was already doing something along the lines of the innovation previous to marketing, and whether there is time available in the agency to permit implementation. It is interesting to observe that the *absence of time* within the agency was of greater moment in affecting utilization than that the agency encouraged or assisted in implementation. In other words, focus and space within one's job were more significant than a climate of support. This suggests, again, that particular attention should be given to practical, job-related aspects of implementation in designing a social product (such as a handbook), in the selection and exploitation of the marketing channel (such as the workshop), and in building in a follow-up, reinforcement scheme within the target market (such as the agency system).

We discover again in this set of data that implementation may be related to characteristics of particular service delivery systems. In this substudy community mental health centers were more inclined to implement than were family service agencies. It may be that certain systems are more innovation prone and receptive to outside inputs than are other systems. It could be that the type of innovation (community strategies) was more relevant to one system than to the other. It may be that the nature of the materials and means of transmission may have been more consistent with norms of one system or the other; for example, sponsorship of the project by NIMH may have influenced community mental health centers. All that can be said with certainty is the truism that different service delivery systems respond differentially to different marketing efforts.

Of lower order, but still relevant, appear to be the attitudes of the agency director. None of these attitudinal variables concerning the agency director emerged as significant. They had moderate to low statistical rankings. The only reason they received rankings at all was that there was no technical reason to leave them out. Only a very slight trend was observed. It might be that we could facilitate utilization to some degree if agencies were selected where directors used decentralized decision making, were receptive to outside ideas, and had a commitment to a community-oriented approach. Diffusion undertakings might be aided somewhat if simple indices were available for classifying agency directors along such dimensions. It should be noted that this was a minor side substudy, and our procedures for gauging these agency director attributes were not strong. Thus a great deal of weight should not be placed on this aspect of the study.

Structural Variables and Utilization

During the course of the study, we were given access to data collected nationally by the FSAA and NIMH. These data concerned such agency structural variables as size of budget and staff, composition of professional staff, and others. While not central to the primary theoretical issues of our study, these data allowed us to explore the interesting question of the extent to which structural features of agencies facilitate or encourage greater use of innovative inputs.

We found 14 structural variables common to both CMHCs and FSAAs, 5 of which were significant at the .05 level or beyond. Highest levels of utilization were positively related to amount of "total expenditures," the number of "professional employees on staff," and a high "ratio of staff to 100,000 population." Higher levels of spending on personnel also had some relation to a high level of utilization, as did the number of professionals in "other" categories associated with an agency.

Utilization would thus appear to be related to agency size, professional staff size and heterogeneity, and a service orientation on the part of the agency as evidenced by intensity of staff coverage. These results are consistent with research literature on diffusion of innovations and with findings of the low-intensity marketing study. We were unable to assess the relative importance of structural variables and more process-type variables in fostering innovation utilization.

Having concluded a high-intensity and a low-intensity social marketing undertaking, it is now possible to make comparative judgments concerning the two approaches. We turn to that intriguing task in the next chapter.

Note

1. Internal samples were overrepresented by respondents from agencies with "high salaries and expenditures" and by respondents from agencies with "high staff/client ratios." These agency types were positively related to utilization. In effect, these two variables, viewed without reference to other factors, could account for some of the positive effect of the internal agent.

In addition, the internal sample was overrepresented by "percentage of social workers." Since a high percentage of social workers was negatively related to utilization, however, this difference could have reduced the positive effect of the internal agents. Similarly, a difference for "percentage of 'other' employees" may have reduced the positive effect of internal agents. In this case, the internal agent sample was underrepresented by respondents from agencies with a high percentage of other professionals. Because a high percentage of other professionals was found to have a positive effect on utilization, the underrepresentation may have reduced the positive effect on the internal sample.

We can summarize the situation in this way: the four problematic agency variables were both significantly different for internal/external agents *and* related to utilization. Each variable's effect on the positive results of the internal agents can be characterized as follows:

percentage of social workers:	decreased positive effect
salary and expenditures:	increased positive effect
staff ratio (by 100M pop.):	increased positive effect
percentage of "other" professionals:	decreased positive effect

References

Abelson, H. I. *Persuasion.* New York: Springer, 1959.

Andrews, F. *Multiple classification analysis.* Ann Arbor: Institute for Social Research, University of Michigan, 1973.

Argyris, C. *Behind the front page.* San Francisco: Jossey-Bass, 1974.

Becker, M. Sociometric location and innovativeness: Reformation and extension of the diffusion model. *American Sociological Review,* 1970, 35(2), 267-282.

Bettinghaus, P. *Persuasive communication.* New York: Holt, Rinehart & Winston, 1968.

Boone, L., & Kurtz, D. L. *Foundations of marketing.* Hinsdale, IL: Dryden, 1977.

Cohen, A. R. *Attitude change and social influence.* New York: Basic Books, 1964.

DeLozier, M. *The marketing communications process.* New York: McGraw-Hill, 1976.

Gluckstern, N. B., & Packard, R. W. The internal-external change agent team: Bringing change to a "closed institution": A case study on a county jail. *Journal of Applied Behavioral Science,* 1977, 13(1), 41-52.

Hage, J., & Dewar, R. *The prediction of organizational performance: The case of program innovation.* Paper presented at the American Sociological Association annual meeting, Denver, Colorado, August 1971.

Havelock, R. G. *A guide to innovation in education.* Ann Arbor: Center for Research on the Utilization of Scientific Knowledge, Institute for Social Research, University of Michigan, 1970.

Havelock, R. G. *The change agent's guide to innovation in education.* Englewood Cliffs, NJ: Educational Technology Publications, 1973.

Havelock, R. G., & Havelock, M. C. *Training for change agents.* Ann Arbor: Center for Research on the Utilization of Scientific Knowledge, Institute for Social Research, University of Michigan, 1973.

Newman, J. W. New insights, new progress, for marketing. *Harvard Business Review,* November/December 1957, p. 100.

Rogers, E. M., & Shoemaker, F. F. *Communication of Innovations.* New York: Macmillan, 1971.

Rothman, J. *Planning and organizing for social change: Action principles from social science research.* New York: Columbia University Press, 1974.

Shaw, S. J. Behavioral science offers fresh insights on new product acceptance. In P. R. Cateora & L. Richardson (Eds.), *Readings in marketing: The qualitative and quantitative areas.* New York: Meredith, 1967.

Watson, G., & Glaser, E. M. What we have learned about planning for change. *Management Review,* November 1965, p. 36.

Zaltman, G., Duncan, R., & Holbek, J. *Innovations and organizations.* New York: John Wiley, 1973.

PART IV

IMPLICATIONS OF
SOCIAL MARKETING

CHAPTER 10

A SOCIAL MARKETING RETROSPECTIVE

Certain aspects of social marketing advocacy have been uncovered in each of the two project studies, which examined high-intensity, high-involvement methods on the one hand and low-intensity, low-involvement approaches on the other. Other interesting and informative conclusions come to light when these two studies are compared. One of these conclusions emphasizes similarities, while the other emphasizes differences between the two studies.

Cross-Study Comparison of
Social Marketing Methods

In retrospect there is a remarkable concurrence in findings in the high-intensity and the low-intensity social marketing field studies—two quite different research situations. Both conclude that level of authority in the organization is not a salient variable in diffusing professional innovations. Hierarchical position was not a significant factor in encouraging dissemination and utilization either in terms of diffusion agent status (executive versus peer) or in terms of mass communication entry into the organization (executive versus middle-level program staff). Likewise, both studies discovered that intraorganizational rather than extraorganizational factors were more powerful in stimulating utilization by professionals of such innovations. The internal workshop leader, compared to the external, was more effective; and appeals were of decreasing impact as the point of reference moved from within the organization to outside its structural boundaries (from Bureaucratic to Professional to Community/Client Appeals).

The question of whether internal or external change agents are of a greater significance in promoting organizational innovation is a controversial and unsettled theoretical issue in the social sciences. These two field studies come down squarely on the internal side. They also straddle the issue of whether authority or peer group opinion leader influences are stronger, suggesting that both are of equal weight.

These conclusions should be read in the context of the particular diffused (or marketed) innovation and the organizational structure of the field agencies. The innovation was a professional tool that could be adopted by individual practitioners without requiring concerted organizational decision making or structural changes. Each staff member was relatively free to incorporate the innovation (one that was complex and required a period of time to implement) into his or her practice situation or to decline to do so.

Dissemination of behavior modification (reinforcement) techniques, for example, may be similar to what was involved here. Practitioners can use reinforcement as a conscious technique in a fairly direct and obtrusive way (giving consistent verbal praise for client behavior that is compatible with intervention objectives). Introducing family therapy into an agency, however, may require various organizational-level decisions and actions. Practitioners' assignments and workloads may be affected, intake workers would be required to change their procedures in allocating cases, spatial layout may even have to be altered, with small conference rooms enlarged and combined to allow for group interaction during sessions. Our point is simply that our study has dealt with conditions associated with the former, individual professional, decision-type innovation.

The other contextual factor pertains to the human relations type of structure that is generally descriptive of the service delivery systems in the study. These are two human service agencies in which professionals provide mental health services to clients and community groups with some degree of discretion— and in a practice setting that does not lend itself to close, hierarchical surveillance. In such settings it would not be surprising to find a blunting of higher-level of authority and to discover that internal collegial influences have some import. We are uncertain whether the results would be comparable for innovations diffused in more extreme authoritarian or centralized systems, such as prisons or factories.

Cost-Benefit Aspects of Social Marketing

There was difference in cost-effectiveness results in comparing the two studies. We were interested, within the boundaries of the study, in taking a look at the question of whether high-intensity or low-intensity approaches are preferable from the standpoint of efficiency.

Our comparative analysis of the cost effectiveness of the two approaches resulted in a *more favorable* assessment of the *low-intensity* program. Excluding fixed costs (the central facility, core personnel, and so on), high-intensity program expenses were approximately double those of the low-intensity program ($8000 versus $4000). These extra costs were used for transportation, per diem for traveling staff, salary for the extra staff we needed to engage, special facilities for workshops, and so on.

The question is, did this doubled expense justify itself in terms of more utilization through the high-intensity social marketing approach? As the same utilization scale items were used for both approaches, we can answer this question with some definiteness. Table 10.1 shows the patterns of use found for all respondents, based on the three levels of utilization employed in both the high- and low-intensity marketing studies.

It is clear that, overall, the high-intensity approach brings about a greater proportion of utilization at the high level (30 percent versus 22 percent). With those participants contacted, it can be said to have a better effectiveness record. However, looking at absolute numbers, it is seen that the low-intensity

TABLE 10.1   Utilization Rates for High-Intensity Study Versus Low-Intensity Study

Study	Low Utilization	Medium Utilization	High Utilization	Total
High intensity				
Number	127	134	113	
%	34.0	36.0	30.0	100
Low intensity				
Number	466	334	223	
%	45.0	33.0	22.0	100

approach resulted in almost twice as many individuals (223 versus 113) employing the handbook guidelines at high levels of utilization. In other words, *for half the cost, the low-intensity approach resulted in twice the amount of high utilization.* Despite its lower cost, the low-intensity approach created 110 more instances of high utilization than did the high-intensity approach. (It is interesting to note that the family service subsample showed *similar percentages* of high utilizers for both approaches, with a slightly greater proportion of high utilizers stimulated under the low-intensity approach.)

This leads to a consideration of the subject of *social* values, *social* costs, and *social* benefits in human service systems. Those of us who are involved in the social realm concentrate on the philosophical dynamics of ethics and morality when we speak of social benefits. Social marketers are, to a greater or lesser extent, also concerned with such questions; but their concern clearly extends also to the area of economics. Human service practitioners, particularly those involved in direct client service and interaction, are usually only tangentially concerned with the economics of social service, perhaps only to the extent that economic considerations enhance or impinge upon their immediate practice situations. Questions of budget, fund allocation and distribution, acquisition of resources, and so forth, are, for the most part, the purview of the agency administrator, board in control, and administrative support staff. Yet, when one begins to define the boundaries of social economics, it begins to become clear that the human service worker, whatever the focus of his or her activities, is inextricably tied to economic forces. A word or two of explanation demonstrates why this is so.

Virtually all economists would tend to agree that economics concerns the allocation of scarce resources among alternative means. We have little difficulty understanding what this may mean in terms of dollars and cents when the resources with which we deal are limited, natural ones. Every industrialized nation in the world—and the citizens of those nations—have, since 1973, seen quite clearly the implications—political, social, and economic—of competing demands for the world's limited and rapidly diminishing petroleum supply. From time to time over the past three decades, efforts have been made to achieve a broad-based understanding of the economic importance of *human* resources. It is this that provides the periodic impetus for human resources accounting, a movement that has yet to make a significant impact on our social system.

One of the difficulties we must deal with when considering human resources (which are as varied as natural resources) is that we are not accustomed to assessing costs, revenues, and profits in other than monetary terms. While economic theories face no such limitation, social theorists and practitioners have only rarely addressed the problem. Yet there are costs in social endeavors, and revenues, profits, and losses. In the social sphere we merely use a different medium of exchange.

The human service practitioner, for example, counts *time* among his or her principal resources. It is a limited resource, unrenewable, that must be allocated carefully among the competing demands of client, agency, family, community, and so on, if the practitioner is to achieve optimum effectiveness; that is, if he or she is to achieve the greatest "good" for client and community. Costs are a measure of the rate at which scarce resources are used up. Revenue, for the human service worker, is a measure of how much "good" he or she can accomplish using the resources available. Social profit is a measure of the extent to which the practitioner's achievements permit him or her to continue the generation of social revenues. Social costs, social revenues, and social profits will vary as a function of both the quantity and quality of demands that are made upon the practitioner's resources.

As a broader, if somewhat simplistic, example, consider the case of two adoption agencies in the same community. Let us assume that one is enormously successful (by whatever criteria we might choose to select) in the placement of children for adoption. The other experiences little or no success. The first will likely experience growth in its available resources (increased funding, increased staffing, and so on) and will maintain itself as a viable social "business." It is operating at a "social profit." The second agency, because it is operating at a "social loss," must in time decline, in size, reputation, fiscal resources, or professional influence.

The paradox of the "successful" social enterprise is that success increases its competition for available resources: People in need gravitate to where their needs can, in their belief, be met. As the competition for resources increases, stress builds in the resource allocation and distribution system. Not only are there costs in the *application* of resources, but in the allocation and distribution of those resources as well. It is this that necessitates an examination of the various marketing modes in order that social products may be taken to their intended markets as cost-effectively as possible.

As a "marketing strategy," the high-intensity approach we examined in the second part of this presentation has been more or less the traditional marketing mode of professionals in the social services. A strong professional bias exists in its favor. It is appealing philosophically because of its high degree of personalization; and, as the human service professions are for the most part person directed, the rationale underlying such a marketing mode appears to be soundly based.

There is, nevertheless, a need to address ourselves to the cost-effectiveness of such a marketing mode. It is clear that as our society becomes increasingly complex, human service needs become correspondingly greater. The demands made upon human service resources appear to be increasing geometrically, while the resources themselves, if they increase at all, appear to do so at best arithmetically. Thus the costs of allocation and distribution of those resources become increasingly important. This gives rise to the necessity for examining other marketing modes in order that we might gain data for assessing the most cost-effective approach for a given marketing problem.

Experience has taught the commercial world that low-intensity marketing approaches (namely, those we generally speak of as "mass marketing") have proved effective for specific (although not all) marketing efforts. In the low-intensity phase of our research, we set out to discover whether or not such an approach might be acceptably cost-effective for some social marketing problems. Our effort was a limited one in which we sought trends, suggestions for further areas of exploration, and indications of circumstances under which low-intensity social marketing might prove nearly as cost-effective as the more traditional, high-intensity effort.

The cost-related results of the field study, in contradiction to our own expectations, forcefully suggest that human service workers and social scientists should apply their keen professional skepticism to their own established ideological preference for interpersonal modes of diffusion. A range of diffusion and social marketing strategies, tied to purpose, resources, target audience, and so forth, should be given cognizance and assessed with a cold, analytical eye. This leads, as well, to considering a promotional mix or marketing mix, wherein different methods are combined to produce maximum effects. That line of research would be a useful addition to current diffusion studies.

Giving Social Marketing Its Due in Applied Social Research

Diffusion requires the same rationality and openness that research requires. Further, keeping faith with one's findings, for the applied social scientist, implies, as we stated initially, a "product advocacy" or "campaign" outlook, carefully articulated with social marketing methods and procedures conducive to user adoption. In other words, the same attention, drive, and competency that goes into formulating a research study or into doing development work must also be given to the design of a plan of diffusion. This entails elements such as:

(a) isolating a universe of practitioners or organizations who are potential target users;

(b) determining key attributes, attitudes, and needs of users;

(c) packaging appropriate materials and appeals in an attractive, responsive way;

(d) reaching and motivating potential users;

(e) locating functional gatekeepers, authority figures, opinion leaders, or informal networks as entry points and diffusion channels;

(f) providing initial training and ongoing support and reinforcement to users; and

(g) developing procedures for scanning results of diffusion strategies.

No reasonable social scientist or human service practitioner would argue that the present tools of our trade are adequate to deal with the huge social and personal problems that come before struggling practitioners and/or administrators in human service agencies. Even when new, research-generated, excellent technologies are developed, these diffuse through the professional infrastructure in a slow and halting fashion. We already know that the lag between the creation of an innovative idea or technique and its widespread application may involve years—even decades—and there are good reasons for that lag. There is comfort and security in using familiar, accepted methods. Extra energy and nagging risk come with trying something new. Ideological barriers, enveloped in traditional thinking, also stand in the way. Furthermore, new methods and procedures are not always guaranteed to work. Changing over to behavior modification forms of mental health treatment, for example, means discarding a half century of Freudian precepts about the nature of human beings and how they may be given assistance.

Research results and their innovative applications need, there-fore, to be conveyed with determination to potential users and beneficiaries if they are not to languish or die.

An important aspect of an affirmative posture toward social marketing relates to the careful preparation of research and development products in forms that are of particular interest and appeal to intended users. As a case in point, the low-intensity study with its large sample revealed a useful piece of information concerning the response to the handbook. A great deal of effort went into packaging the handbook for subsequent social marketing, with regard both to content and to format. In the evaluation form, respondents were asked to indicate their positive or negative reactions to this social product. The percentages of respondents checking "favorable" or "very favorable" responses to handbook attributes were as follows:

Item	% checking "very favorable" or "favorable"
applicable to my agency	94.6
applicable to my job	84.3
clear, concise, easy to read	89.9
not too technical	89.1
overall reaction	75.6

The staff interpreted these results to be generally supportive of the rationale behind the handbook, particularly the princi-ples for communicating that went into its construction. We also found a statistically significant relationship between degree of favorableness toward the handbook and depth of its utilization. Care in communicating research and research-derived products is obviously not a trivial matter.

We hope that our study has amplified three elements of meaningful diffusion and social marketing: (1) a proactive pos-ture in carrying the innovative fruits of development out into the world of the user; (2) a conscious, empirically based evalua-tion of means of reaching users by testing reactions; and (3) a well-thought-out, strategic plan for diffusion. These are the conventional methods of marketing in the industrial sphere (promotional activity, test marketing, strategic marketing). Adapting them to the social sphere—selectively, and with proper attention to the different operational and value considerations in the two fields—may offer much potential for making social science more relevant and influential, especially as applied to human services.

Questions may be raised concerning various aspects of our particular diffusion program. These might include whether the types of appeals used and tested were most salient, whether the variables of workshop leadership that were examined are the most pertinent, whether direct mailing is the most appropriate means of announcing an innovative package, whether the measurement tools were adequate, and so forth. These matters can, indeed, be debated and subjected to further research. This should be done, we feel, in the context of, and toward advancing, social marketing concepts and methods.

There is, at best, a tenuous connection between social research and social practice that results in neither deriving the full potential benefit of input and feedback from one to the other. Our research effort is an attempt to advance the process of identifying those significant factors that enhance communication and utilization. We know more now than we knew when we began about several of these factors: appeal and entry as applied to the human services, and locus and status of personal diffusion agents. In time we will refine our knowledge of these and other factors; but we have now, at least, a point of departure in advancing our understanding of the social marketing process.

APPENDIX A
Brochures with Reference Group Appeals

THE BUREAUCRATIC APPEAL

Responsibilities
Promoted by
Mental Health Agencies
and How To Master Them

Mastering Systems Intervention Skills

A Handbook for Community Mental Health and Family Service Professionals

---

The National Institute of Mental Health, the Family Service Association of America, and other important mental health agencies have urged increased responsibility for work with community groups and institutions.

These mental health agencies have increased their concerns in the areas of community psychology, community psychiatry, and community organization. Policies and programs of these agencies encourage preventative programs.

Practical Techniques for Effective Work With Community Groups

Preventative mental health — family and child advocacy — mobilizing community resources — family life education — community outreach: Whatever your responsibilities may be, this Handbook offers practical techniques and advice for meeting them.

This handbook will be helpful in two distinct areas. First, it can guide you in establishing innovative services for families in the community. Second, it can provide you with strategies for fostering effective community participation in services, programs, and decision-making.

Live examples, written by practitioners, of their experiences in implementing guidelines

A planning guide for laying out a specific strategy and course of action

Concrete action guidelines based on research and practice

Advice and precautions from skilled practitioners

Step by step techniques of implementation

This 62-page Handbook is the product of six years of practical research—a six year field experience in human service agencies. NIMH funding makes possible its free distribution—to you and your agency colleagues.

Reply:

The Mental Health Community Intervention Project is a non-Profit Service and Research Program, based at the University of Michigan, and sponsored by the National Institute of Mental Health.

Please send copies of the Handbook for me and my agency colleagues, whose names I have listed below:

Name:

Agency:

Address:

City:

State: Zip:

Quantity Desired:

Agency Colleagues:

(You may order up to twelve copies for the staff of your agency.)

THE MENTAL HEALTH COMMUNITY INTERVENTION PROJECT

THE PROFESSIONAL APPEAL

Responsibilities
Promoted by
the Mental Health Professions
and How To Master Them

FAMILY AND
CHILD ADVOCACY

FAMILY LIFE
EDUCATION

PREVENTATIVE
MENTAL HEALTH

OUTREACH

MOBILIZING
COMMUNITY
RESOURCES

Mastering Systems Intervention Skills

A Handbook for Community Mental Health and Family Service Professionals

The mental health professions have urged increased responsibility for active work with community groups and institutions.

Professional associations have increased their concerns in the areas of community psychology, community psychiatry, and community organization. Current professional literature encourages preventative programs.

Practical Techniques for Effective Work With Community Groups

Preventative mental health — family and child advocacy — mobilizing community resources — family life education — community outreach: Whatever your responsibilities may be, this Handbook offers practical techniques and advice for meeting them.

This handbook will be helpful in two distinct areas. First, it can guide you in establishing innovative services for families in the community. Second, it can provide you with strategies for fostering effective community participation in services, programs, and decision-making.

Live examples, written by practitioners, of their experiences in implementing guidelines

A planning guide for laying out a specific strategy and course of action

Concrete action guidelines based on research and practice

Advice and precautions from skilled practitioners

Step by step techniques of implementation

This 62-page Handbook is the product of six years of practical research—a six year field experience in human service agencies. NIMH funding makes possible its free distribution—to you and your agency colleagues.

Reply:

The Mental Health Community Intervention Project is a non-Profit Service and Research Program, based at the University of Michigan, and sponsored by the National Institute of Mental Health.

Please send copies of the Handbook for me and my agency colleagues, whose names I have listed below:

Name: _____

Agency: _____

Address: _____

City: _____

State: _____   Zip: _____

Quantity Desired: _____

Agency Colleagues:

_____

_____

_____

(You may order up to twelve copies for the staff of your agency.)

THE MENTAL HEALTH COMMUNITY INTERVENTION PROJECT

Responsibilities
Promoted by
Community Groups and Key Citizens
and How To Master Them

FAMILY AND CHILD ADVOCACY

FAMILY LIFE EDUCATION

PREVENTATIVE MENTAL HEALTH

OUTREACH

MOBILIZING COMMUNITY RESOURCES

Mastering Systems Intervention Skills

A Handbook for Community Mental Health and Family Service Professionals

---

The National Association for Mental Health, the Child Welfare League, and other important voluntary community organizations have urged increased responsibility by professionals for active work with Community groups and institutions.

Together with key political leaders, concerned community people support developments in the areas of community psychology, community psychiatry, and community organization. And, they encourage preventative programs.

Practical Techniques for Effective Work With Community Groups

Preventative mental health — family and child advocacy — mobilizing community resources — family life education — community outreach: Whatever your responsibilities may be, this Handbook offers practical techniques and advice for meeting them.

This handbook will be helpful in two distinct areas. First, it can guide you in establishing innovative services for families in the community. Second, it can provide you with strategies for fostering effective community participation in services, programs, and decision-making.

Live examples, written by practitioners, of their experiences in implementing guidelines

A planning guide for laying out a specific strategy and course of action

Concrete action guidelines based on research and practice

Advice and precautions from skilled practitioners

Step by step techniques of implementation

This 62-page Handbook is the product of six years of practical research—a six year field experience in human service agencies. NIMH funding makes possible its free distribution—to you and your agency colleagues.

Reply:

The Mental Health Community Intervention Project is a non-Profit Service and Research Program, based at the University of Michigan, and sponsored by the National Institute of Mental Health.

Please send copies of the Handbook for me and my agency colleagues, whose names I have listed below:

Name: _____

Agency: _____

Address: _____

City: _____

State: _____   Zip: _____

Quantity Desired: _____

Agency Colleagues:

_____

_____

_____

(You may order up to twelve copies for the staff of your agency.)

THE MENTAL HEALTH COMMUNITY INTERVENTION PROJECT

APPENDIX B
Follow-Up Questionnaire on Utilization—
Low-Intensity Study

Reactions to the Handbook on Mastering Systems Intervention Skills for Community Mental Health and Family Service Professionals

A. With regard to the Handbook on MASTERING SYSTEMS INTER-VENTION SKILLS, please *check all categories below* that apply to your experience with this Handbook.

1. _____ I did not receive a copy of the Handbook.

2. _____ I received a copy of the Handbook.

3. _____ I examined the Handbook.

    4. _____ read it.

    5. _____ studied it.

6. _____ After examining the Handbook, I later thought about or referred back to it.

7. _____ After examining the Handbook, I seriously considered applying it to my practice.

8. _____ I applied some of the concepts from the Handbook, either in a formal or informal manner.

9. _____ I partially implemented a specific action guideline (stopped before completing tasks of implementation)

    10. _____ but did not use the Handbook in a systematic way (did not refer back to it or fill out an Initial Log Form)

    11. _____ used the Handbook in a systematic way (referred back to it and filled out an Initial Log Form).

12. _____ I fully implemented a specific action guideline (completed tasks of implementation)

    13. _____ moderately attained the goal (less than 75% goal attainment)

    14. _____ largely attained the goal (75-100% goal attainment).

B. For this section, please check or complete the appropriate category.

1. Age _____

2. Sex: Female _____   Male _____

3. Check the highest degree received:

_____ High School diploma (or equivalency)   _____ Ph.D.
_____ Bachelor   _____ M.D.
_____ Master   _____ M.D. and Ph.D.
_____ D.S.W.   _____ Other. Please
                                                      specify_____

4. How long have you held your current job title? _____ (years)

5. How long have you been involved professionally in the human service field? _____ (years)

6. My main professional identity is (please check ONE only):

_____ Education   _____ Psychiatry   _____ Social Work
_____ Medicine   _____ Psychology   _____ Sociology
_____ Nursing   _____ Public Health   _____ Business
_____ Public Relations
_____ Other. Please specify: _____

7. The Handbook's content:

	Strongly Agree	Agree	Disagree	Strongly Disagree
a. Is applicable to the work of my agency	____	____	____	____
b. Is applicable to my job	____	____	____	____
c. Is clear, concise, easy to read	____	____	____	____
d. Is not too technical, given its jargon	____	____	____	____

8. My overall reaction to the Handbook was:

_____ Favorable
_____ Somewhat favorable
_____ Neutral
_____ Somewhat unfavorable
_____ Unfavorable

9. What factors presented obstacles to completing a guideline?

_____ Time
_____ Money/Lack of resources
_____ Not considered part of job role/Not relevant to my work
_____ Did not have a copy of Handbook available
_____ Insufficient assistance given in Handbook
_____ Personal factors
_____ Lack of support from administrator/agency
_____ Lack of support from colleagues
_____ Lack of support from supervisor
_____ Not favorable to guidelines
_____ Already have similar guidelines
_____ Other. Please specify: _____
_____

10. Please explain items checked in question 9.

Please enclose this reactionnaire in the envelope provided and mail to:
MENTAL HEALTH COMMUNITY INTERVENTION PROJECT
1015 East Huron
Ann Arbor, Michigan 48109

APPENDIX C
Depth of Utilization
Questionnaire Development

We undertook an extensive review of the diffusion and marketing literature to find evaluation instruments dealing with the extent of utilization of innovations. While a complete listing of all studies reviewed is neither practical nor productive, we can say that only a very few assisted in devising the type of questionnaire we desired.

We then consulted with expert resource persons. Everet Rogers, perhaps the leading authority in the field of diffusion of innovations, informed us in a personal communication that published studies of diffusion typically evaluate only up to the point of deciding to adopt an innovation. For the most part, actual degree of utilization has not been evaluated. This was reconfirmed in conversations with Louis G. Tornatzky, coauthor with G. W. Fairweather of numerous books on innovation in mental health settings.

Existing literature, however, was *suggestive* in a number of ways. For example, it was instructive to review the Coleman et al. study (1966) of medical innovations (see References, Chapter 7). In that study, questionnaire emphasis was related to the physician's web of communication. The degree of utilization was measured by the number of prescriptions written for a certain new drug, and this was determined by searching the prescription files of pharmacists. The procedure was interesting but only marginally useful to the specific questionnaire design task in our work.

Another interesting study, using an interview and self-administered questionnaire to examine the degree of utilization of an educational innovation, was conducted by Gross et al. (1971; see References, Chapter 7). A case study method was employed to gauge the implementation of a new role definition for schoolteachers. The emphasis was on personal and situational motivation accounting for using the innovation, with little attention to delineating actual degrees of utilization. However, the study indicated possible background variables to include in our questionnaire.

Overall, the literature sources were useful mainly in suggesting a wide range of background questions related to the personal attitudes and attributes of practitioners, organizational variables, and the characteristics of the handbook. Even the most interesting sources reviewed, however, were only marginally useful in terms of our objective: the measurement of the depth of utilization of an innovation. We found it necessary to develop our own set of measurement tools.

As the literature search had produced a broad set of interesting contingency variables that might be related to utilization, it began to appear that a lengthy questionnaire would have to be produced. We realized that mental health professionals were typically heavily overcommitted in work tasks. We had no wish to add to their burden more than necessary. For this reason, we devised a series of short subquestionnaires to be given in two stages. Two initial scanning questionnaires reviewed the respondents' general experiences with the workshop and handbook. These were followed by a set of appropriate "probe" or follow-up questions, tailored to a specific practitioner's specific experience. For example, only those respondents who had indicated problems with the handbook received probe questionnaires asking them to specify such problems. We felt that this approach was economical of the respondents' time and that it would stimulate a greater response rate.

Altogether, our initial instrument consisted of seven subquestionnaires:

(1) *Questionnaire A.* This provided information about whether the practitioner had criticisms of the handbook or the workshop, and whether or not he/she had implemented a guideline.

(2) *General Background Questionnaire.* This was designed to determine personal attributes of practitioners and was administered simultaneously with Questionnaire A.

(3) *Probe Questionnaire I.* This determined factors that discouraged use of the handbook. It was requested only of those who had indicated criticism or nonuse of the *handbook* in Questionnaire A.

(4) *Probe Questionnaire II.* This was designed to assess difficulties with the workshop experience and was administered to those practitioners who stated some criticism of the *workshop* in Questionnaire A.

(5) *Probe Questionnaire III.* This was aimed at determining what factors were associated with incomplete implementation of a guideline. It was administered to those who indicated in Questionnaire A that they had *initiated but not completed an implementation.*

(6) *Questionnaire B.* This was designed to determine the extent of depth of utilization for those who stated that they *had begun to carry out a guideline.*

(7) *Questionnaire C.* This was designed to describe the guideline-specific details of how practitioners had actually *implemented a particular guideline.*

Two pretests assessed the instrument. The prime focus of these pretests was determination of whether practitioners were able to respond to the various types of questions asked of them and, in particular, to be sure that their responses to Questionnaire B did indicate the depth of utilization of the handbook strategies.

The first pretest was informal. Telephone interviews were held with 12 practitioners who had previously asked to use the handbook for exploratory purposes on a voluntary basis. As we progressed, it became clear that a telephone interview procedure was not an efficient method for reaching the large number of individuals planned for the final sample. We adopted a more formal, written procedure for the second pretest, contacting the participants by mail.

The second pretest was conducted with 20 participants of a continuing education workshop at the 1974 Spring Symposium at the University of Michigan. During a 2-day program, these 20 were introduced to the guidelines through a "bread board" version of the handbook. Shortly after the symposium, the practitioners were asked to respond to a set of 2 questionnaires, mailed at 2 different times. Initially they received the first-phase scanning questionnaires. About 6 weeks later they were sent the individually responsive probe questionnaire(s). Phone calls and postcard reminders encouraged participants to complete and return the questionnaires.

We had experimented with two separate mailings of short questionnaires with the expectation that individuals would be more likely to complete two shorter questionnaires than a single longer one. Contrary to expectations, the attrition rate of participants from the first to the second mailing was heavy. We decided, therefore, to use one fairly lengthy questionnaire as the final evaluation procedure. The questionnaire would be designed with clearly marked skip patterns to enable respondents to answer only those questions appropriate to their situation. The second field test provided additional useful information on wording of items, item spacing, instructions for proceeding through the questionnaire, and so forth.

We designed the questionnaire in sections, as follows:

Section A: the workshop experience and reaction to it

Section B: the handbook—experience with and reaction to it

Section C: personal background information—age, sex, education, professional background, etc.

Section D: general activities in implementing guidelines

Section E: specific details of implementation of *Participation* guideline

Section F: specific details of implementation of *Innovation* guideline

Section G: factors within the organization that prevented or encouraged utilization

Throughout questionnaire development, the objective of measuring the respondent's depth of utilization was kept in the forefront. As stated, this measure was conceived of as a continuum; a respondent's score along that continuum represented the highest level of utilization carried out by that individual. By this means we could make comparisons of how far individual practitioners, agencies, and other subgroups had gone in implementing a guideline.

The original depth of utilization scale consisted of nine items, scattered throughout the questionnaire. These nine and the response distribution of the actual study were as follows:

Item	*Frequency*
skimmed or read handbook	79
studied handbook	9
thought about or referred back to handbook	20
considered implementation	53
applied concepts in practice	82
partially implemented a guideline	87
partially implemented in a systematic manner	4
implementation success in outcome: 0 to 75%	15
implementation success in outcome: 76 to 100%	7
Total	356

We originally drew up the items based on the logic of the process of utilization and on our examination of the general literature. As a result of the pretests, the wording and arrangement of the items were modified and evolved into these nine.

Because of very low frequencies in some of these categories, it appeared that it would be a more meaningful scale if those levels were combined with adjacent categories. Specifically, only 9 (2.5%) of the 356 respondents studied the handbook but did nothing further. It was obvious, therefore, that nearly all of those who studied the handbook also exhibited further utilization on the continuum.

The seventh category, "partially implemented a guideline in a systematic manner," also contained a very low number of practitioners. Thus those who went so far as to preplan their effort and begin a systematic implementation actually carried it out further.

These low category frequencies suggested the possibility of collapsing the scale to improve the distribution of the dependent variable, Depth of Utilization (DU). Most of the DU analysis was to be completed through the use of contingency tables. This becomes problematic when any cell of the tables has very low frequencies, for the statistical tests used in such table analysis are dependent upon sufficiently large cell frequencies.

As a result of the unfavorable distribution on the nine-point Du scale, several revisions were attempted. The first of any consequence was a seven-point Du scale consisting of the following:

Item	Frequency
skimmed handbook	45
read or studied handbook	43
thought about handbook or referred back	20
considered actual implementation of the handbook	53
applied concepts in practice	82
partially implemented a guideline	91
fully implemented a guideline	22
Total	356

This scale increased the validity of the chi square and maximum likelihood statistics. The cell size requirement was met for almost all of the analysis variables. Exceptions were those independent variables with many categories, such as agency and region. As analysis progressed, however, additional problems with this particular scale became apparent. There is a tendency for otherwise linear relationships between many specific independent variables and depth of utilization to be interrupted or reversed at the fifth category, "applied the concepts in practice." In addition, we thought that problems with this particular category might be accounting for the rather low gamma and tau B ordinal measures we obtained.

We decided to experiment with a DU scale collapsed into a three-point scale: low, medium, and high. This division could be used to verify that significant findings were due to actual differences among categories and not to the random variations that can occur if categories are nondistinct; that is, if categories actually measure overlapping levels of utilization. A three-point scale resulted.

For this revision of the DU scale, 18 respondents who had been categorized previously as "missing data" (scored zero on the DU scale) were reclassified. In our statistical analysis, it was impossible to determine from the score of zero whether a respondent simply failed to complete the questionnaire or whether, in fact, that respondent experienced "no activity" with regard to the handbook. We decided that such persons would be included with those whose highest level of utilization was skimming the handbook. Respondents for whom we had no additional data (those who failed to complete the questionnaire) would automatically be left out of any two-way contingency table analysis, as the data would also be missing on the independent variable.

The new three-point scale was as follows:

Item	Frequency
Low—skimmed handbook, read handbook, referred back or thought about it further	113
Medium—considered implementation or actually applied concepts in practice	142
High—partially or fully implemented a guideline	119
Total	374

The results of a two-way analysis of this distribution using the three-point scale confirmed the findings of the seven-point scale; that is, findings that were statistically significant using the seven-point scale continued to be significant using the three-point scale. The strength of the relationships, as evidenced by ordinal statistical scores (gamma and tau B), exhibited an increase.

One area of concern still remained. The percentage of explained variance was undesirably small. Again, we looked at the DU scale as a possible contributor to this situation. The original fifth category, "applied it to my practice," produced uneasy feelings, and we suspected it was too general. This raised the specter of respondents being categorized as "medium" utilizers when they were, in reality, "low" handbook utilizers. If we were right, the amount of explained variance would increase if this category were eliminated. All respondents, therefore, whose highest level of utilization had been the fifth category were reclassified and allowed to fall on the scale where they would have fallen if that specific question had not been included.

The elimination of the fifth category and the reclassification of the zero scores produced the following six-point scale:

Item	Frequency
no activity, or skimmed the handbook (includes some who failed to complete the questionnaire)	74

read or studied the handbook	68
referred back or thought further about the handbook	41
considered implementation of a guideline	92
full implementation of a guideline	21
total	374

The consequences of this new scale were dramatic. Not only did the ordinal statistic measuring strength of relationship between the independent variables and the DU increase, but the linear trends were much clearer, with fewer reversals evident.

Based on these results, a second and final three-point scale was developed:

Item	Frequency
Low—no activities, skimmed, or read handbook	127
Medium—studied, referred back to, thought further about, or considered use of handbook	134
High—partial or full implementation of a guideline	113
Total	374

The gamma and tau B relationships between independent variables and the DU appeared even stronger. Trends were even more clearly defined.

Further documentation that this three-point scale yielded the most satisfactory DU measures was provided by examining the multiple R (multivariate correlation statistic) and multiple R^2 (the explained variance). These both exhibited significant increases.

In summary, the final form of the DU scale provided the most consistent and interpretable findings. It was the measure of the dependent variable used in analysis.

APPENDIX D
Supplementary Data—Low-Intensity Study

Section I: CMHCs—Personal and
Organizational Variables

Appeal			Probability Level
Bureaucratic	Professional	Community/Client	Chi Square $p =$

Large Catchment Areas

.50	.41	.36	.47

High Number of Professional Employees

.58	.43	.34	.39

High Number of Full-Time Social Workers

.52	.46	.34	.01

Low % of Full- and Part-Time Social Workers

.51	.44	.40	.03

High % of Full- and Part-Time Social Workers

.53	.46	.40	.04

Only two significant stratified results were obtained that did not follow this established pattern:

Low % of Minority Staff

.53	.52	.55	.06

High Number of Professional Employees in "Other" Category

.44	.46	.37	.04

Section II: Both Systems—Statistically Significant Variables

Appeal			Probability Level
Bureaucratic	Professional	Community/Client	Chi Square $p =$

High Expenditures

.52	.47	.35	.01

High Number of Professional Employees

.54	.44	.38	.02

High Number of Full–Time Social Workers

.54	.43	.36	.05

High Number of Professional Employees in "Other" Category

.49	.44	.38	.05

High Salaries and Related Expenses

.52	.50	.37	.04

High Ratio of Staff/100,000

.54	.49	.39	.03

Section III: CMHCs—Practitioner Demographics and Agency Characteristics

Appeal			Probability Level
Bureaucratic	Professional	Community/Client	Chi Square $p =$

Low Age Group

.63	.64	.54	.04

High Age Group

.60	.61	.60	.05

High Number of Years in the Human Services

.57	.65	.56	.03

Large Catchment Areas

| .57 | .62 | .53 | .00 |

Low Number of Full-Time Social Workers

| .60 | .63 | .53 | .04 |

Large Number of Nongraduate Social Workers

| .59 | .61 | .52 | .02 |

Low Staff Ratio

| .57 | .62 | .52 | .02 |

Three significant results indicated that, for selected CMHC practitioners, particularly those with a lower degree of professional involvement, a Bureaucratic Appeal should encourage utilization:

B.A. and Lower Degree

| .67 | .61 | .58 | .01 |

Low Number of Years in the Human Services

| .66 | .60 | .58 | .05 |

Low % of Minority Staff

| .60 | .53 | .51 | .01 |

Section IV: Both Systems—Practitioner Demographics and Agency Characteristics

Appeal			*Probability Level*
Bureaucratic	*Professional*	*Community/Client*	*Chi Square* $p =$

Low Age Group

| .64 | .62 | .56 | .04 |

B.A. or Lower Degree

| .69 | .60 | .59 | .01 |

Low Number of Years in the Human Services

.66	.60	.58	.05

Low % of Minority Staff

.62	.56	.53	.01

High Number of Full–Time Social Workers

.61	.60	.54	.02

High Number of "Other" Professionals

.60	.59	.55	.03

APPENDIX E
High-Intensity Sample Characteristics

	a	b	c	d	e	f	g	h	i	j	k
Treatment 1: Internal Authority											
CMHC	6	112	60	53.6	103	32	29	9	8	72	64.3
FSAA	2	35	31	88.6	34	1	3	1	2.8	31	88.6
Total	8	147	91	61.9	137	33	22	10	6.8	103	70
Treatment 2: Internal Peer											
CMHC	6	100	59	59	93	18	18	7	7	62	62
FSAA	3	51	22	43.1	51	12	24	0	0	37	72.5
Total	9	151	81	53.6	144	30	20	7	4.6	99	65.6
Treatment 3: External Authority											
CMHC	7	117	51	43.6	107	32	27	10	8.5	84	71.8
FSAA	2	33	25	75.8	33	4	12	0	0	29	87.9
Total	9	150	76	50.7	140	36	24	10	6.7	113	75.3

Treatment 4: External Peer

	a	b	c	d	e	f	g	h	i	j	k
CMHC	9	217	99	45.6	175	42	19	35	16.1	165	76.0
FSAA	2	46	27	58.7	41	9	20	5	10.9	37	80.4
Total	11	263	126	47.9	216	51	19	40	15.2	202	76.8

Totals: All Treatments

	a	b	c	d	e	f	g	h	i	j	k
CMHC	28	546	269	49.3	478	124	22/7	61	11.1	383	70.1
FSAA	9	165	105	63.6	159	26	15.8	6	3.6	134	81.2
Total	37	711	374	52.6	637	150	21	67	9.4	517	72.7

a = number of agencies that conducted a workshop
b = subjects—individuals receiving a follow-up questionnaire. Had been listed to receive a handbook or were recorded as attending a workshop (filled out aregistration and/or reactionnaire).
c = number of questionnaires returned; i.e, respondents
d = % of questionnaires returned from subjects (b)—c/b
e = number of individuals listed originally by agency to receive a handbook and attend a workshop
f = number of individuals listed by agency (as in e) but who were not recorded as attending a workshop—f/b
g = % of "subjects" in b who were not recorded as attending a workshop—f/b
h = number of individuals who were recorded as attending a workshop, but were not on original agency list (e)
i = % of subjects in (b) who were recorded as attending a workshop but were not on the original agency list (e)—h/b
j = number of individuals recorded as attending a workshop (i.e., filled out a reactionnaire)
k = % of subjects (b) who were recorded as attending a workshop (j)—j/b

APPENDIX F
Agency Director Innovativeness Questionnaire

Questionnaire on Organizational Attributes
of Community Mental Health Directors

Please characterize agency directors with respect to the following administrative attributes. Your reactions are those of an outside objective observer who is looking in to view the operations of the agency. Base your response on executives you know of currently functioning in agencies across the country; don't limit your base of comparison to a particular region or city.

Decision Making (We are dealing here with the director's attitude toward involving a broad cross-section of staff in decision making.)

1. _____ The director regularly makes decisions himself; staff is consistently not involved.

2. _____ The director makes most decisions himself; staff is involved occasionally.

3. _____ The director and the staff share about equally in decision making; he makes some and they make some.

4. _____ The director bases most of his decisions on staff views; decision making is largely staff determined.

5. _____ The director bases his decisions regularly on staff views; decision making is consistently staff determined.

_____ No opportunity to observe; lack of information or no opinion.

Receptiveness to Outside Ideas (Receptiveness means real listening and considering, not a "political" pose. Outside means external to the formal structure of the agency or its funding sources.)

1. _____ The director is receptive to all new ideas from outside his agency.

2. _____ The director is receptive to a large number of new ideas from outside his agency.

3. _____ The director is receptive to a moderate number of new ideas from the outside.

4. _____ The director is receptive to relatively few new ideas from outside his agency.

5. _____ The director is not receptive to any new ideas from outside his agency.

_____ No opportunity to observe; lack of information or no opinion.

Community Oriented

1. _____ Strong commitment to a community oriented approach, including community outreach and involvement.

2. _____ Somewhat strong commitment to a community oriented approach, including community outreach and involvement.

3. _____ Moderate commitment to a community oriented approach, including community outreach and involvement.

4. _____ Somewhat weak commitment to a community oriented approach, including community outreach and involvement.

5. _____ Weak commitment to a community oriented approach, including community outreach and involvement.

_____ No opportunity to observe; lack of information or no opinion.

APPENDIX G
Standard Workshop Format

Basic Components of the Workshop

Introduction of self (others)

Identification with the project (expert or peer)

Purpose and background of the project (see below for outline)

Rationale for diffusion-workshops; desire of funder to see handbook used rather than stored in the library

Preview of format and schedule for the workshop (what participants should anticipate):
    Emphasis on participation guideline.
    Review of the main ideas behind the strategy.
    Explanation of the log forms.
    Planning a common intervention from the group.
    Work on log in pairs.
    Report back from pairs.
    Very general review of innovation guideline.

Participation Guideline
    Review of the Guideline:
        The benefits notion: sociologically derived, but relevance to behavior modification.
        Four types of benefits.
        The basic pattern of implementation.
        Some obstacles to implementation as expressed by field study practitioners.
    Explain log form.
    Select a participation problem from the group.
    Apply log jointly to the problem.
    Ask group in pairs to work on a real participation problem, using log (serve as consultant to pairs).
    Report back from pairs.

Innovation Guideline
  Quick review of the action principle, how log would be used in implementation.

Any problems in moving ahead with handbook and logs

Project Follow-Up of Implementation
  We will follow up to see how it went and to evaluate different diffusion methods—anticipate questionnaires in [six months].
  Purpose of follow-up is to determine most effective ways of diffusing new practice tools in the field.

Conclusion
  Thank participants.
  Indicate additional handbooks are available upon request by writing project headquarters.

Basic Points About the Purpose and Background of the Project
  — funding
  — based at the University of Michigan
  — seven years of development work
  — started out by searching research for findings on improving community-related work of agencies
  — findings consolidated and converted into action guidelines
  — field tested by practitioners in a range of social welfare and human service agencies and evaluated for outcome effectiveness
  — handbook composed to help other practitioners gain from the experiences of those in the field studies
  — funder now interested in seeing the handbook diffused to professionals and put to use in agencies, rather than placed on a library shelf
  — distribute Project Fact Sheet beforehand, so that this review can be brief

NAME INDEX

SUBJECT INDEX

ABOUT THE AUTHORS

Jack Rothman is Professor in the School of Social Work, University of Michigan. He has been a researcher, teacher, and practitioner in the human services for over 25 years. A continuing theme in his work has been the systematic application of social science knowledge to contemporary issues of policy and practice. He holds a Ph.D. in social psychology from Columbia University and an M.S.W. from Ohio State University. He is the author of 13 previous books; his main areas of writing have included organizational innovation and change, community organization, and race and ethnic relations. He has been a recipient of the Gunnar Myrdal Award for Distinguished Research in Human Services of the Evaluation Research Society.

Joseph G. Teresa, Ph.D., is a Division Director in the U.S. Department of Education, responsible for management efficiencies in organizational analysis. He is an Adjunct Professor at the University of Maryland in organizational evaluation and quality control and productivity. He previously taught at the University of Michigan in the School of Social Work. He is a nationally recognized researcher in the area of organizational management and has published extensively in that field. He consults with public agencies and private corporations in management administration.

Terrence L. Kay is Mathematical Statistician at the Naval School of Health Sciences, Bethesda, Maryland. His current research efforts include the development of techniques to monitor hospital performance and to allocate resources to medical treatment facilities. His educational background includes a master's degree from the the University of Michigan School of Social Work.

Gershom Clark Morningstar is a consultant in mass media matters to corporations and individuals. President of Wolverine-Morningstar Broadcasting, Inc., he is recognized as a national expert in commercial broadcasting material and market research. He has a master's degree in mass communications from the University of Michigan, and has taught at Ithaca College, Eastern Michigan University, and the University of Michigan. He has also served as a researcher in the behavioral sciences and as a media consultant to different units of the federal government.